Conflict Resolution after the Pandemic

In this edited volume, experts on conflict resolution examine the impact of the crises triggered by the coronavirus and official responses to it.

The pandemic has clearly exacerbated existing social and political conflicts, but, as the book argues, its longer-term effects open the door to both further conflict escalation and dramatic new opportunities for building peace. In a series of short essays combining social analysis with informed speculation, the contributors examine the impact of the coronavirus crisis on a wide variety of issues, including nationality, social class, race, gender, ethnicity, and religion. They conclude that the period of the pandemic may well constitute a historic turning point, since the overall impact of the crisis is to destabilize existing social and political systems. Not only does this systemic shakeup produce the possibility of more intense and violent conflicts but also presents new opportunities for advancing the related causes of social justice and civic peace.

This book will be of great interest to students of peace studies, conflict resolution, public policy, and International Relations.

Richard E. Rubenstein, J.D., is University Professor of Conflict Resolution and Public Affairs at George Mason University and is a long-time faculty member and former director of the Carter School.

Solon Simmons, Ph.D., is Associate Professor of Conflict Analysis and Resolution at George Mason University with a Ph.D. in sociology.

Routledge Studies in Peace and Conflict Resolution
Series Editors: Tom Woodhouse and Oliver Ramsbotham
University of Bradford

The field of peace and conflict research has grown enormously as an academic pursuit in recent years, gaining credibility and relevance amongst policy makers and in the international humanitarian and NGO sector. The Routledge Studies in Peace and Conflict Resolution series aims to provide an outlet for some of the most significant new work emerging from this academic community, and to establish itself as a leading platform for innovative work at the point where peace and conflict research impacts on International Relations theory and processes.

Multi-level Reconciliation and Peacebuilding
Stakeholder Perspectives
Edited by Kevin P. Clements and SungYong Lee

The Colombian Peace Agreement
A Multidisciplinary Assessment
Edited by Jorge Luis Fabra-Zamora, Andrés Molina-Ochoa, and Nancy Doubleday

Conflict Resolution after the Pandemic
Building Peace, Pursuing Justice
Edited by Richard E. Rubenstein and Solon Simmons

Theorising Civil Society Peacebuilding
The Practical Wisdom of Local Peace Practitioners in Northern Ireland, 1965–2015
Emily E. Stanton

For more information about this series, please visit: www.routledge.com/ Routledge-Studies-in-Peace-and-Conflict-Resolution/book-series/RSPCR

Conflict Resolution after the Pandemic

Building Peace, Pursuing Justice

**Edited by Richard E. Rubenstein
and Solon Simmons**

Routledge
Taylor & Francis Group

LONDON AND NEW YORK

First published 2021
by Routledge
2 Park Square, Milton Park, Abingdon, Oxon OX14 4RN

and by Routledge
52 Vanderbilt Avenue, New York, NY 10017

Routledge is an imprint of the Taylor & Francis Group, an informa business

© 2021 selection and editorial matter, Richard E. Rubenstein and
Solon Simmons; individual chapters, the contributors

The right of Richard E. Rubenstein and Solon Simmons to be
identified as the authors of the editorial material, and of the authors
for their individual chapters, has been asserted in accordance with
sections 77 and 78 of the Copyright, Designs and Patents Act 1988.

British Library Cataloguing-in-Publication Data
A catalogue record for this book is available from the British
Library

Library of Congress Cataloging-in-Publication Data
A catalog record for this book has been requested

ISBN: 978-0-367-72199-2 (hbk)
ISBN: 978-0-367-72201-2 (pbk)
ISBN: 978-1-003-15383-2 (ebk)

Typeset in Times New Roman
by Apex CoVantage, LLC

Contents

Author bios   viii
Foreword   xi

**Introduction: the crises of 2020 and the field of
conflict studies**   1
RICHARD E. RUBENSTEIN AND SOLON SIMMONS

**PART I
Conflict resolution in a period of social crisis**   7

1 **Big peace: an agenda for peace and conflict studies
   after the coronavirus catastrophe**   9
   SOLON SIMMONS

2 **Lessons from disaster: history and the current crisis**   17
   PETER N. STEARNS AND RICHARD E. RUBENSTEIN

3 **From the frying pan to the fire: environmental crises
   and their implications for conflict resolution**   24
   MICHAEL SHANK

**PART II
Global political conflicts after the pandemic**   33

4 **Pandemics, globalization, and contentious politics**   35
   AGNIESZKA PACZYNSKA AND TERRENCE LYONS

5 **Migration and the COVID-19 pandemic** 43
OMAR GRECH

6 **COVID-19 and nationalism** 51
KARINA V. KOROSTELINA

7 **A new global covenant? Great power conflicts and conflict resolution in the post-corona era** 61
MOHAMMED CHERKAOUI

PART III
Intergroup conflicts after the pandemic 71

8 **The triple crisis: reevaluating socio-economic values in a period of social reconstruction** 73
MICHAEL D. ENGLISH

9 **Racial justice in a post-COVID America: toward systemic conflict resolution and peacebuilding** 81
ARTHUR ROMANO

10 **The gendered frontlines: perpetuated inequalities or a reimagined future** 89
SHEHERAZADE JAFARI

11 **Internal and eternal insecurity: impact of crisis on religious group identity** 97
CHARLES DAVIDSON

PART IV
Conflict resolution initiatives after the pandemic 105

12 **Peace engineering in a complex pandemic world** 107
ALPASIAN ÖZERDEM AND LISA SCHIRCH

13 **COVID-19 amidst conflict** 115
ODED ADOMI LESHEM

14 **When elephants roar: the coming moral conflict
    between the United States and China**   123
    GAO QING

    Concluding note   130
    SOLON SIMMONS AND RICHARD E. RUBENSTEIN

    Index   134

Author bios

Editors

Richard E. Rubenstein, J.D., is University Professor of Conflict Resolution and Public Affairs at George Mason University and is a long-time faculty member and former director of the Carter School. He is the author of nine books on resolving social conflicts, including *Resolving Structural Conflicts: How Violent Systems Can Be Transformed* (Routledge, 2017).

Solon Simmons, Ph.D., is Associate Professor of Conflict Analysis and Resolution at George Mason University with a Ph.D. in sociology. He is a specialist in narrative and its relation to peacebuilding, and his most recent book is *Root Narrative Theory and Conflict Resolution; Power, Justice and Values* (Routledge, 2020), which provides researchers and practitioners tools grounded in cutting edge approaches to narrative and conflict.

Contributors

Mohammed Cherkaoui, Ph.D., is an adjunct professor of conflict resolution and peacebuilding at George Mason University's Jimmy and Rosalynn Carter School for Peace and Conflict Resolution and has written extensively on conflict issues in the MENA region and elsewhere.

Charles Davidson, Ph.D., is Research Faculty at the Carter School for Peace and Conflict Resolution at George Mason University and is the Executive Director of its Political Leadership Academy. He has spent 11 years engaging in research and peacebuilding efforts around the world, including projects in Asia, Africa, and Latin America

Michael D. English, Ph.D., is Associate Director and Core Instructor for the Peace, Conflict, and Security Program at the University of Colorado Boulder. He is the author of *The United States Institute of Peace: A Critical History* (Lynne Reinner, 2018) and other works.

Omar Grech is a Maltese lawyer and is the Director of the Centre for the Study and Practice of Conflict Resolution at the University of Malta. He has written extensively on human rights and serves as Lecturer within the Department of International Law.

Sheherazade Jafari, Ph.D., focuses on gender, religion, and human rights in conflict and peacebuilding. She is the Director of the Point of View International Retreat and Research Center at the Carter School for Peace and Conflict Resolution, George Mason University.

Karina V. Korostelina, Ph.D., is the Director of the Program on History, Memory, and Conflict at the Carter School for Peace and Conflict Resolution. Her research on identity-based conflicts, reconciliation, and the role of memory and history in conflict and post-conflict societies has been presented in more than eighty articles and sixteen books.

Oded Adomi Leshem is a Postdoctoral fellow at the Harry S. Truman Research Institute for the Advancement of Peace and at the Psychology of Intergroup Conflict and Reconciliation Lab of the Hebrew University. He is an adjunct professor at the Carter School for Peace and Conflict Resolution and has published widely on the psychology of peace processes.

Terrence Lyons, Ph.D., is Associate Professor at the Jimmy and Rosalynn Carter School for Peace and Conflict Resolution. He received his Ph.D. from Johns Hopkins University and was a Fellow at the Brookings Institution and the Peace Research Institute, Oslo. His publications include *The Puzzle of Ethiopian Politics* (2019) and *Politics from Afar: Transnational Diasporas and Networks* (2012).

Alpasian Özerdem, Ph.D., is Dean of the Jimmy and Rosalynn Carter School for Peace and Conflict Resolution, and Professor of Peace and Conflict Studies at George Mason University. Professor Özerdem has published extensively, and most recently is the co-editor of *Comparing Peace Processes* (Routledge, 2019) and the *Routledge Handbook of Peace, Security and Development* (2020).

Agnieszka Paczynska, Ph.D., is Associate Professor at the Carter School for Peace and Conflict Resolution, George Mason University. Her publications include *Conflict Zone, Comfort Zone: Ethics, Pedagogy, and Effecting Change in Field-Based Courses* and *The New Politics of Aid: Emerging Donors and Conflict Affected States*.

Arthur Romano, Ph.D., is Assistant Professor at the Carter School for Peace and Conflict Resolution and is a certified Kingian nonviolence trainer and consultant. He has published original research on community responses to police violence and systemic racism in the United States.

Lisa Schirch, Ph.D., is North American Research Director for the Toda Institute for Global Peace and Policy Research, Senior Policy Advisor with the Alliance for Peacebuilding, and Research Professor at the Center for Justice and Peacebuilding at Eastern Mennonite University.

Michael Shank, Ph.D., is the Communications Director for the Carbon Neutral Cities Alliance, committed to achieving long-term carbon reduction goals. He teaches graduate courses on *Sustainable Development, Power and Politics* and *Climate and Security* at NYU, and *Communicating Conflict* at George Mason University.

Peter N. Stearns, Ph.D., is University Professor of History at George Mason University. He has written widely on the history of peace and world history, more generally, with a new edited volume on the modern history of death appearing shortly.

Gao Qing is the Executive Director of the Confucius Institute U.S. Center in Washington, DC. He received the Master of Science degree from Carter School for Peace and Conflict Resolution at George Mason University in 2007.

Foreword

According to many visions of the future, the post-pandemic world is a bleak place shaken by deep tremors in the political and economic world order. It is a world of fear, uncertainty, isolationism, authoritarian governance, and socio-economic catastrophes. The trauma of the pandemic, the widespread anxiety that it has produced, and its visible tendency to exacerbate social and political conflicts can be projected forward to produce a grimly dystopian view of world society.

On the other hand, paradoxically, there is also a genuine hope in many communities that humanity can learn significant lessons from the ills of how we lived, consumed, and ran our societies before the pandemic. Coexisting with dystopian fears there is a strong belief that humanity can use this crisis as an opportunity to build a better world based on the lessons learned from the "old normal." An apocryphal story has it that the Chinese word for "crisis" is composed of characters that mean both "danger" and "opportunity." The story may be fictitious, but the concept is convincing. A crisis such as the current pandemic generates both justifiable fears and equally justifiable hopes.

What is to prevail for the future from this binary of projections is yet to be seen. It seems clear, however, that unless we address deep-rooted structural challenges such as the global injustices of decision-making, trade, and finance, the "old normal" will return with additional socio-economic challenges, such as increased unemployment, deeper gaps between the haves and have-nots, and wider societal divisions. Without needed changes, the post-pandemic world is likely to be a much harsher environment for preventing conflict and building peace, because the security and development challenges faced by many societies around the globe will likely be magnified. Moreover, there may be less political will and fewer resources to deal with them, especially in the international context.

There are already all signs of worsening intercommunity and interstate relations across the world, including protests and counter-protests for racial justice in the United States, deteriorating refugee–host community relations in Europe, inter-religious attacks in India, maritime and energy resources wrangling in Eastern Mediterranean, and increasing political violence in many parts of the Middle East and Africa. To respond effectively in such an environment, the peace and conflict studies community, among others, may need to concentrate on spearheading the post-pandemic change process, expanding on its multi- and interdisciplinary frameworks, and building partnerships for meaningful impact on the ground.

Once the pandemic's immediate impact lessens and the situation becomes more "habitual" over the next few months, the hopeful "lessons-to-be-learned" agenda could lose its attractiveness. Subsequently, returning to the "old normal" might, unfortunately, become more appealing. With that kind of comforting tendency, many people may be tempted to engage in scapegoating: attributing responsibility for endemic environmental and social problems to groups or institutions other than their own. The scapegoats could differ from country to country; migrants or allegedly immoral or extremist groups might play that role in some nations, while in others devious external actors could be targeted. For some groups, China is already such a target, since it is where the pandemic started in early 2020.

If we in the peace and conflict studies community do not want scapegoating to further dominate the political agenda, then we need to be active agents in the facilitation of change in socio-economic and political affairs, from our immediate communities to global relations. Our analyses will have to go deep beneath the surface of events to explore the impact on social relations of institutionalized greed, arrogance, brutality, and ignorance. Our current concerns and research areas in conflict prevention and peacebuilding should serve as useful starting points, but from curriculum development to research, the interface between peace and justice should also become much more explicit. In this way, we can turn spotlights on how such fundamental issues as the unsustainable exploitation of nature, bad governance, social inequality, discrimination, and many other injustices based on race, gender, faith, caste, and sexuality negate the formation of peaceful relations.

There is currently flourishing energy for transformative change globally, but to place this in a sound framework and to progress effectively we need, first, to focus on root causes. Second, we need to gather better evidence on what works in preventing conflicts and building peace. Third, we should help to organize responses to these challenges as proactive actors of conflict resolution and transformation. For example, the peace and conflict studies community could coordinate partnerships between universities, think tanks, civil society organizations, activists, social movements, and governments as facilitators and drivers of change. Overall, our community has an excellent opportunity to be bold, innovative, and relevant in responding to a truly global challenge.

Furthermore, to deal with the wide range of socio-economic and political impacts of the pandemic, the work of peace and conflict studies needs to become even more interdisciplinary than it is at present. Peace and conflict studies already benefit from the interfaces of various social sciences such as anthropology, political science, psychology, and sociology with such fields as philosophy, history, and religious studies. There is now a tendency to move forward toward an even more transdisciplinary approach in which disciplinary boundaries merge so that peace and conflict studies can be perceived as a "discipline" in its own right. A wide range of schools, institutes, and centers worldwide demonstrates these different contours of interdisciplinary and transdisciplinary perspective. Such diversification is, in fact, a point of richness and advantage in terms of how individual peace and conflict studies institutions can engage with the post-pandemic world.

Having said this, though, I would still urge the peace and conflict studies community to open their doors to STEM (Science, Technology, Engineering, and Math) disciplines, as well. For a long time, these disciplines were considered to be wedded to the sociopolitical and military status quo. Nevertheless, in order to remain relevant to new peace and security challenges, our work must benefit from technology and STEM research methodologies, systems, and tools. On the ground, this is already happening; for example, technology (including "big data") is used extensively in early warning systems, refugee crises, and conflict prevention systems. However, there is still much room for further engagement with STEM disciplines in our teaching and research. It is ironic that peace engineering or humanitarian engineering activities are often hosted in engineering schools rather than in peace and conflict studies institutions.

Finally, peace and conflict studies programs have built strong partnerships with local peacebuilding actors. There has been significant growth in local ownership and participation methodologies in peace and conflict studies research. Many of our colleagues now teach such bottom-up approaches in conflict prevention and peacebuilding. For example, the concept of "everyday peace" has emerged from the desire to understand peace as a daily occurrence phenomenon rather than a macro level objective: the absence of political violence. To create a meaningful impact on the ground, however, the peace and conflict studies community still needs to improve its practice in several ways.

First, a meaningful impact depends upon meaningful partnerships. In turn, these can be achieved only through building trust between the parties, a process that requires adequate time to nurture transformative relationships. Second, the peace and conflict studies community in the global

North still needs to eradicate asymmetric power relations with partners in the global South. Especially in the aftermath of the pandemic, we are likely to end up with a much more vulnerable global South due to the pandemic's negative impacts on socio-economic resources and capacities. Finally, our work with local peacebuilding networks should be used in efforts to rebuild pandemic-affected societies. There are likely to be many opportunities for such transitioning, which could lay the foundations for more multi- and interdisciplinary applications.

With these post-pandemic world challenges in mind, the members of George Mason University's Jimmy and Rosalynn Carter School for Peace and Conflict Resolution are eager to take an active role both in research and education and in forging new practical partnerships. The Carters' legacy of selfless, brave, and insurmountable dedication to peace has been our beacon in the process of renaming our school. Their name affirms that we pursue a particular set of values: compassion, humility, solidarity, a calling for social justice, and a commitment to peace. Those values matter for us, because we are a community of doers who have dedicated ourselves to preventing conflict and building peace while pursuing social justice, both locally, nationally, and internationally.

This book has been motivated by such a sense of ethical activism. Its co-editors, Professors Richard E. Rubenstein and Solon Simmons, its contributors, and the other members of our broad community of scholars and activists hope to initiate a post-pandemic peace and conflict studies conversation about our field's roles, responsibilities, and future trajectories for teaching, research, and practice. As the Carter School, we hope that the publication of these short essays written by faculty members, researchers, alumni, and other colleagues will stimulate a broader discussion leading to concrete steps to shape peace in the post-pandemic world.

The peace and conflict studies community is well placed to play a leading role in the challenging drama that humanity is currently experiencing. With our skills of facilitation, negotiation, mediation, and understanding and experience of how to resolve and transform conflicts, we have a responsibility to engage with these problems. Our societies hunger for this sort of leadership in building peace and pursuing justice. For institutions like ours to remain relevant, we need to act as active agents of transformative change.

Alpasian Özerdem

Introduction

The crises of 2020 and the field of conflict studies

Richard E. Rubenstein and Solon Simmons

The outbreak of the coronavirus and global spread of the disease COVID-19 in the spring and summer of 2020 shocked and frightened the world. The shock was particularly disconcerting, however, in relatively prosperous, advanced industrial nations that had long considered themselves immune from such ancient dangers. With the advantage of hindsight, one can see that the plague was not the only recent threat to human security that seemed strangely antediluvian. Rather than experiencing the nuclear exchanges and cyberwars feared by many experts, nations rich and poor were afflicted by natural disasters, many linked to climate change, that appeared almost biblical in their scope and effects: earthquakes, cyclones, fires, and floods. But in important respects, the pandemic was even more devastating, since it was followed by a series of aftershocks that intensified and extended the crisis.

To begin with, combating the virus meant quarantining populations and imposing new controls over the social behavior of large numbers of people. The immediate effects of such measures were to suspend normal business activities, generating massive losses of capital and jobs, to curtail internal and international travel, and to close schools and places of public accommodation. The results soon began to resemble the effects of the Great Depression of the 1930s, with workers, poor farmers, and people of color bearing the brunt of the economic damage, as well as suffering disproportionate losses from the COVID-19 plague itself. Moreover, as it became clear that authoritative figures and institutions in a number of nations had failed to secure their people against these biological and economic threats, the relations between citizens and authorities were subjected to enormous strain. In the United States and certain other nations, the shocks of medical vulnerability, economic decline, and exacerbated inequality were compounded by militant (although largely nonviolent) movements of protest challenging the systems that had allegedly failed to secure people's basic rights and interests. Protests and demonstrations organized by groups on the left emphasized the role of political and economic institutions and attitudes in perpetuating racism, sexism, and other forms of structural and cultural inequality, while those emanating from the right emphasized threats to individual freedom posed by bureaucratic authorities and scientific experts.

For researchers in the field of conflict analysis and resolution, the successive shocks of the pandemic and ensuing conflicts constituted a major challenge. Although it was not clear that the crisis had generated new social struggles, it seemed undeniable that it had inflamed existing conflicts, especially those between antagonistic socio-economic, political, and cultural groupings. What, then, could be said about the likely course of these struggles? Would they expand and escalate? Would new opportunities for peaceful conflict resolution be presented? The scholars' attempts to project existing trends into the near-term and middle-term futures were complicated by two further features of this unusual crisis: the rise of radical uncertainty and the delegitimization of established governance systems.

Radical uncertainty

Normally, advanced industrial nations rely heavily on short term planning that assumes the predictability of everyday events. (The stock phrase, "business as usual" reflects this assumption). But the pandemic and its aftershocks undermined predictability, making it virtually impossible to say when the virus would be brought under control, how it could be expected to develop pending the development of an effective vaccine, or when economic and social activity in affected nations could safely resume. In fact, as the crisis continued throughout 2020 with no end in sight, the uncertainty increased and became more general. People's expectations that social and political relations would return to some "normal" status quo ante tended to erode. Analysts assumed that the coronavirus would eventually disappear as a major public health problem, but many came to believe that post-corona society would be altered in fundamental respects. For example, serious environmental threats would almost certainly continue to cause destruction and alarm the public as a result of ongoing climate changes, creating demands for protective and preventative government action not unlike those made in response to the COVID-19 crisis. Meanwhile, the inability of private and public organizations to make reliable short-term plans played havoc with the economy, as well as with many people's sense of personal stability.

Delegitimization of governance systems

The failure of established leaders and institutions to deal effectively with the pandemic and its sequelae constituted another shock, especially in economically advanced nations that had long considered themselves models of effective public administration and responsible citizenship. As the United States became the global epicenter of the pandemic, accounting for more than one-quarter of all coronavirus cases and COVID-19 deaths, U.S. residents found themselves observing governance systems in nations such as China, Vietnam, and South Korea with envy and incomprehension. Utilizing a combination of top-down state authority and bottom-up popular collectivism, these regimes apparently brought the virus under control, as did certain European states that could rely on relatively efficient administrations and disciplined populations. But from the United States and Brazil to India and the Philippines, in nation after nation that failed to deal adequately with the pandemic and its economic consequences, relationships between ruling elites and subject groups were seriously disrupted, as were relations between scientific and technical experts and masses of people now unsure about what or whom to believe.

Pre-pandemic political and social systems were clearly impacted by the crisis, although it is not yet clear how profound and long-lasting these changes will prove to be. Of particular importance to conflict analysts are the implications of changes that alter or bypass existing institutions intended to manage social conflicts, since this sort of disruption can open doors both to escalated struggles and to new peacemaking initiatives. For example, the current burst of demonstrations and other activities on behalf of racial justice in the United States could conceivably generate a white nationalist backlash that, exploited by unscrupulous or desperate political leaders, might make violent confrontations such as the Charlottesville, Virginia riot of 2019 seem commonplace. Alternatively, one can imagine the present strong surge of public support for organizations protesting police violence generating a new popular consensus that could support multiracial peacebuilding in the United States on a large scale. In short, to maintain that the pandemic of 2020 and its aftershocks have very likely inflamed existing social and cultural conflicts by no means forecloses the possibility that, by shaking up existing systems of governance, they have also created new opportunities for effective conflict resolution.

With these thoughts in mind, the editors of this volume invited selected colleagues in the field of conflict studies to write about the pandemic's impact on social conflicts which they have studied or tried to resolve, and the likely course of these conflicts in the post-pandemic period. This was a challenging task not only because of the general uncertainties noted earlier but also because periods of recovery from historical crises tend to be especially volatile. In the depths of an environmental, economic, or political crisis, people struggle to regain their psychological balance and to deal with the immediate threats presented by a radically altered environment.

But, as the situation changes and elements of recovery make themselves felt, attitudes and behaviors change as well. Hope reappears, and with it, anger and impatience. Paths to the future that seemed entirely obscured now glimmer seductively, and activist social currents begin to flow, ending the period of mass paralysis. Especially, considering that periods of recovery from major crisis are often lengthy, halting, and uneven, what should conflict specialists say about the prospects for intergroup conflict and peace after the pandemic?

In preparing to answer such questions, the contributors to this volume were encouraged to put aside the common cautionary attitude that discourages scholars from projecting current trends into an uncertain future. Instead, understanding that they were helping to begin a discussion, not to utter its last words, they willingly embraced the risks of engaging in "educated speculation." In a Concluding Note that follows the last of these essays, we will have something more to say about the insights that such an approach can produce. For the moment, we would emphasize that these authors, taken together, constitute a model of multidisciplinary interests and expertise. The disciplinary backgrounds represented here range from political science, sociology, and history to social psychology, law, engineering, environmental studies, cultural studies, and religious studies, all now oriented toward the understanding and resolution of deep-rooted social conflicts. Furthermore, as the essays themselves make clear, the work of these contributors individually and collectively bridges the gap between the theory and practice of peacebuilding.

Three editorial preferences governed the selection of the contributions to this volume:

First, the editors determined that the book as a whole should express a global perspective and should examine the pandemic's likely impact on transnational, not just local, conflict and conflict resolution trends. For this reason, they solicited essays on such topics as climate change, transnational peacebuilding, nationalist vs. globalist struggles, international migration, great power competition, contentious politics and authoritarianism, and the history of multinational crises. This same focus, which transgresses the customary boundary between "international" and "domestic" studies, also guides the research and teaching efforts of the Carter School for Peace and Conflict Resolution, the academic home of a number of the contributors.

Second, hypothesizing that social conflicts are likely to escalate where crises such as the pandemic exacerbate social inequality, make marginalized groups conscious of unsatisfied needs, and frighten more secure or privileged groups, we solicited essays on current and potential intergroup conflicts involving vulnerable social formations. This produced the contributions to the present volume on class struggle, gender-related conflict, race-related conflict, and conflicts involving religious organizations. In keeping with the general thrust of this book, the authors explored not only the possibilities that such conflicts might escalate, but also the opportunities that periods of crisis and recovery might present for breakthroughs to peace.

Finally, the authors were strongly encouraged to engage in "educated speculation" about the likely course of conflicts after the pandemic and the possibilities of resolving or mitigating them in the mid-term and long-term future. Several essays produced in response to this challenge outlined new possibilities of dealing with conflicts visibly escalating under the pressures of the interrelated biomedical, economic, and political crises. Two authors presented a meaningful, wide-ranging discussion of "peace engineering"; a third brought the insights of social psychology to bear on Israeli-Palestinian relations; and a fourth offered a unique process-oriented perspective on the intensifying conflict between the U.S. and China. In addition, innovative methods of conflict resolution in response to systemic changes were discussed in contributors' explorations of a "big peace" perspective, "regenerative" methods of conflict resolution, possible United Nations reforms, and the use of conflict resolution methods in building anti-racist coalitions.

Considering the overall editorial direction of this study, a central organizing principle has been the perception that serious combined crises of the sort that now afflict global society disrupt existing sociopolitical, economic, and cultural systems sufficiently to create new possibilities of both conflict escalation and conflict resolution. The hypothesis that generates discussion in virtually every chapter is that the post-pandemic world will be one in which heightened dangers of increased intergroup and international violence will coexist with promising new opportunities for peacemaking and peacebuilding. Our authors agree that world society is unlikely to return to "normalcy" featuring minor changes in intergroup and international relations. Most of them are more optimistic than pessimistic about the possibilities of achieving mitigation, if not resolution, of social conflicts exacerbated by the crisis. In any event, reading these essays should assist both students of conflict and general readers to understand that the period of recovery from the current crisis is likely to present us with choices of lasting consequence – opportunities to make things better or worse that require serious consideration now.

Part I

Conflict resolution in a period of social crisis

1 Big peace

An agenda for peace and conflict studies after the coronavirus catastrophe

Solon Simmons

Exposing deep structural problems in the global institutional order, the disruptions of the coronavirus plague demand that we rethink the concept of peace and subject key institutions to question. Much like the recent turn to "the local," "the everyday," and the celebration of little p peace by sociologically inspired peace theorists, the concept of a Big Peace raises questions of radical inclusion that were once unthinkable, and challenges identity in ways that could push us closer to justice or toward the abyss. In the wake of the current series of crises, a revival of interest in the concepts of big peace is predictable.

It seems clear that this moment of global crisis will touch on every aspect of peace and conflict studies, from the boundaries and duties of the nation and state to the scope of human rights and the reach of rule of law, and from systems of business and economic distribution to definitions of personhood and the dynamics of identity formation. To match the matter of the moment will require us to think big, beyond the no longer adequate technocratic approaches to peace and conflict resolution that have become typical of the field for more than a generation.

In this essay, I introduce an agenda for peace and conflict studies that I call "big peace," a concept that is, at once, more historical and more ambitious than has been typical of the field as it has developed in the wake of the Cold War and the fall of the Soviet Union. This big peace agenda is not meant to displace or limit the good work already going on in the field, and its major features should already be really quite familiar, but it has long been clear that the concept of peace has been narrowing and specializing, thereby losing the weight of the older questions of a big peace agenda of the late nineteenth and early twentieth centuries. Although this narrowing of the concept of peace is nothing new, the global pandemic has accelerated the processes that call for its expansion.

To get a sense of what is missing from our current peace agenda and why I think it is so important to expand it in this moment of global crisis, consider two exhibits from the history of international affairs. The first is excerpted from President Franklin Delano Roosevelt's public prayer of June 6, 1944, on the D-Day invasion:[1]

> *With Thy blessing, we shall prevail over the unholy forces of our enemy. Help us to conquer the apostles of greed and racial arrogancies. Lead us to the saving of our country, and with our sister Nations into a world unity that will spell a sure peace a peace invulnerable to the schemings of unworthy men. And a peace that will let all of men live in freedom, reaping the just rewards of their honest toil.*

When Roosevelt delivered that prayer, the United States had not yet been formally part of an international organization designed to secure the peace of the world. After famously inventing the idea of the League of Nations, the United States refused to join it, only being drawn into a similar enterprise in consultation with the British as a second world war was imminent in 1941, coining the phrase United Nations as part of a "fight for freedom" around the world.

Let's pause for a moment to note that the United Nations itself is, in a very concrete sense, a result of the peace movement, a peace movement with big plans for world peace that grew out of collective attempts to limit the uses of war in pursuit of conquest and, as Alfred Nobel put it in his will, to promote "fraternity among nations." These were the ambitions of the field of peace and conflict studies, such as it was, in the early middle of the twentieth century. What is hard to remember after the development of the powerful peace organizations that we now enjoy is that they once had to be invented at all, and that their inventors were the peace scholars, both theorists and practitioners, of the late nineteenth and early twentieth centuries.

The second excerpt is also associated with the United Nations, but this time from the Sustainable Development Goals of the organization that were set in 2015. Way down at the bottom of the list of 17 goals is SDG 16,[2] which is the box into which the representative organization for the world places today's peace and conflict work. Here is the text describing the goal of that work: "Promote peaceful and inclusive societies for sustainable development, provide access to justice for all and build effective, accountable and inclusive institutions at all levels."

These are noble objectives, but they are not nearly as lyrical as the words of Alfred Nobel's will.[3] To get a sense of what this more limited sense of peace and conflict work might mean, we can look to the specific targets and indicators of SDG 16, which range from reducing homicide, human trafficking, and illicit financial transactions to promoting participatory decision-making and public access to information. Again, all worthy goals, but when we define peace in this very limited way and compare it to what it meant to those who formulated the Kellogg-Briand Peace Pact in 1928, when the great powers conspired to outlaw the very notion of war,[4] or in 1945 when it provided the inspirational framework for an organization designed to prevent global catastrophe by inventing the United Nations, or again in 1948, when this new world peace organization set out to define a universal definition of human rights that would apply around the world, we see how much the peace agenda has narrowed during the past century.

To plan what will come after the liberal peace will require that those of us in the field of peace and conflict resolution begin again to think in terms as broad and ambitious as previous generations once did. We need to think broadly about what peace is, how it is related to the major institutional forms of violence and their likely presentations, and how these forms of violence can be constrained in a world in which the West will no longer be able to impose its whims on the rest of the world. In short, we need a big peace agenda in some ways like the one that engendered the Nobel Peace Prize, the League of Nations and the UN, the very notion of international cooperation, and universal human rights, but this time touching on domestic issues as well in a way that includes the nearly eight billion of us.

A science of leftovers?

One of the distinctive features of the field of peace and conflict studies, especially in those forms that have fallen under the label peacebuilding, is that they can be thought of as a kind of science of leftovers.[5] No doubt, Boutros Boutros-Ghali's acclaimed Agenda for Peace was a visionary document for its time,[6] and the subject matter of peacebuilding is in no way unimportant. Still, rather than providing a broad structure within which to situate the range of rival domestic political projects of contending nations, peace in this formulation has tended to develop as a kind of narrow specialization within the broader fields of comparative political science and international relations, albeit one that borrows heavily from sociology and anthropology. Peace as peacebuilding is important work, but it tends to leave the big questions like global stability, the mode of production, forms of government, and rule of law unanswered, borrowing frameworks from presumably more rigorous fields. Peacebuilding therefore tends to become an ideologically narrow frame of reference, while the concept of peace, itself, like justice, is as broad as we should ever want it to be.

In contrast, the big peace agenda demands that we place those major institutional dynamics at the heart of our study, just as in the period prior to the so-called first great debate in international relations peace which was imagined so broadly.[7] Although they didn't use contemporary terms like structural and cultural violence to describe their interests, economists like Norman Angell, journalists like Alfred Fried, lawyers like William Randall Cremer, novelists like Bertha von Suttner, theologians like Nathan Söderblom, social workers like Jane Addams, and diplomats like Elihu Root considered the full range of human institutions in their concepts of peace. These were big peace theorists who imagined a new domain of global human experience that could be characterized either as peaceful or not. It was a project for imagining the future of a truly global and inclusive civilization. They demanded that new institutions be created that addressed the various forms of violence that placed the world at risk of deadly conflict. Their efforts spanned the entire range of sustainable development goals, and the peacemakers of yesterday would have found the tight specialization of our conception of the field to be disastrously narrow, missing the main fault lines of what we now call radical disagreement and deep-rooted conflict.[8]

After all, what should demand more of our scholarly attention and technical expertise than the broad goal of world peace? Should the pursuit of such a thing be consigned to those things that the economists, the humanitarians, the doctors, the political scientists, the other established professionals cannot do or find uninteresting? Should the scholarship of peace remain a science of leftovers when the consensus of the world, such as it ever was, may be falling apart?

Assuming the answers to these questions are no, what sort of imagination would we require to build this bigger peace agenda? At a minimum, we need a way of speaking about peace in relation to the various forms of violence, and with this a clear sense of how the concept of peace is related to the concept of injustice and to the various forms of politics. After all, who among us doesn't believe our own era's popular slogan, "No justice, no peace"? It is far too easy to caricature peace theorists as appeasers and accommodationists, but peace work is often highly conflictual. Justice and peace are highly complementary concepts.[9] The tough talk of those who celebrate self-interest and selfishness actually lets those thinkers off the hook; they rarely have to consider what comes after the violence or the victory – what it means to sit in power as yourself a perpetrator of perceived injustice, and how the violence necessarily employed in pursuit of a clear version of justice might turn the page of the book of complex future escalations and principled reprisals.

Security is not a right-wing issue. A big peace agenda would necessarily address the problems of nuclear weapons, standing armies, failed states, and terrorist bands, and much of big peace scholarship would focus as much on the global north as it does the global south. Big peace researchers and practitioners would need to develop win–win orientations, strategies, and tactics for the major security challenges facing the world, and they would need to bring those security concerns into domestic agendas as well, as these touch on issues of racism, bigotry, and economic inequality. They would need to reimagine security much as those who advocate to "defund the police" demand in the United States – as a challenge to the moral imagination as much as to fiscal calculation. These concerns that I have elsewhere labeled "securitarian" deserve close attention from the field's leading lights, just as they received in previous eras of big peace thinking.

Democracy matters, too. Where it was once commonplace for lawyers and democratic theorists to play leading roles in thinking about peace, today, it is far less common to pose basic questions about form of government, rule of law, and the meaning of human rights in relation to the future of peace. It should be obvious, but democratic elections and peaceful transitions of power are among the greatest conflict resolution devices ever invented, and the same could be said for courts of law and their careful procedures to protect and ensure due process – in other words individual human rights. These are "liberal" institutions of peace worth preserving (even when they are often based on adversarial methods of dispute resolution and power politics), and their role in building the institutions of the coming peace should sit at the center of our discipline. This aspect of liberalism in relation to peace should remain central, even as the more properly labeled "neo-liberal peace" loses its hegemony

Bring back class analysis. Peace studies grew up in the aftermath of the Cold War, and the last thing its founding practitioners wanted to do was go back to the bad old days of ideological struggle and the shadow of mutually assured destruction. These concerns led to vagueness and evasion when it came to the big economic questions.[10] This is a problem because structural violence, although a valuable idea as were many big ideas developed in the ideological shadow of the Cold War,[11] tends to appear in our analyses in a way as to obscure our view of the stakes of the struggle over economic power, political economy, and economic institutions. Where are our analyses of public goods and the welfare state in relation to peace? Thomas Piketty raised the alarm about the 1% and its use of real estate as a weapon in the coming struggles to dominate the world economy, but what do we as peace theorists have to say about that instrument of injustice?[12] Health disparities are cruel demonstrations of racial conflict and colonial history, but are they anchored in more prosaic rules through which we manage scarcity. We need also to reach back to an earlier era, prior to the Pax Americana and the Cold War, to ask basic questions about the future of peace whose answers include data-driven questions about economics, power, property, and business. These are not the sorts of things that serious peace scholars of our generation can dodge as many of those before us did.

Finally, we need to think anew about the symbolic boundaries of human experience and human dignity. A big peace perspective's native soil concerns diversity, inclusion, equity, and respect for all people, their heritage and their identity, and these concerns relate to abuses and violence in their own right, not just as forms of cultural violence (read ideology) that support some other objective structure that we mark off as structural violence.[13] As Nancy Fraser implies,[14] a big peace agenda would recognize disrespect, hatred, and status structures as distinctive forms of abusive, systemic power, while simultaneously asking questions about how the symbolic group boundaries we rely upon break us into factional prisoners of the crimes of our ancestors. In a sociological spirit, it would interrogate the distinctions we draw to define gender and sexuality and those between ethnic and racial categories, allowing us to recognize the horrors of all forms of bigotry around the world as we have slowly come to do in the global north.

Conflict is global in the same sense it was in the late nineteenth century but more thoroughly so. The big peace scholars of that earlier era who fashioned institutions for disarmament, humanitarian aid, refugee policy, universal rights, and a kind world parliament in the United Nations must be our guides. Our moral imaginations must touch on concerns broad enough to speak to security in the face of our power to do physical harm, liberty in the face of the power of government coercion, equality in the face of the powers of economic exploitation, and dignity in the face of the powers of abuses of status systems and social privilege. Peace is a concept too big to be left to a narrow academic specialization. Our thoughts about peace must be as large as the social forces that threaten it, newly emboldened by the global pandemic. This is why the time for big peace has returned.

Notes

1 Roosevelt, "D-Day Prayer."
2 United Nations, "About the Sustainable Development Goals."
3 Nobel, "The Will."
4 Hathaway and Shapiro, *The Internationalists.*
5 Commentary Magazine, "A Science of Leftovers."
6 Boutros-Ghali, "An Agenda for Peace."
7 Ashworth, "Did the Realist-Idealist Great Debate Really Happen?"; Quirk and Vigneswaran, "The Construction of an Edifice"; Schmidt, *International Relations and the First Great Debate.*
8 Lederach, "Sustainable Reconciliation in Divided Societies"; Ramsbotham, *Transforming Violent Conflict*; Ramsbotham, "Is There a Theory of Radical Disagreement"; Simmons, *Root Narrative Theory and Conflict Resolution.*
9 Lederach, *The Moral Imagination.*

10 Rubenstein, *Resolving Structural Conflicts*.
11 Galtung, "Violence, Peace, and Peace Research"; Burton, *Conflict*; Boulding, *Three Faces of Power*.
12 Piketty, "Capital in the 21st Century."
13 Galtung, "Cultural Violence."
14 Fraser, "Rethinking Recognition"; Fraser, *Scales of Justice*.

References

Ashworth, Lucian M. "Did the Realist-Idealist Great Debate Really Happen? A Revisionist History of International Relations." *International Relations* 16, no. 1 (2002): 33–51.

Boulding, Kenneth E. *Three Faces of Power*. Newbury Park, CA: Sage Publications, 1989.

Boutros-Ghali, Boutros. "An Agenda for Peace: Preventive Diplomacy, Peacemaking and Peace-Keeping." *International Relations* 11, no. 3 (1992): 201–18.

Burton, John W. *Conflict: Human Needs Theory*. London: Palgrave Macmillan, 1990.

Commentary Magazine. "A Science of Leftovers." June 1, 1947. www.commentarymagazine.com/articles/reader-letters/a-science-of-leftovers/.

Fraser, Nancy. "Rethinking Recognition." *New Left Review* 3 (May–June 2000).

———. *Scales of Justice: Reimagining Political Space in a Globalizing World*. Vol. 31. New York: Columbia University Press, 2009.

Galtung, Johan. "Cultural Violence." *Journal of Peace Research* 27, no. 3 (1990): 291–305.

———. "Violence, Peace, and Peace Research." *Journal of Peace Research* 6, no. 3 (1969): 167–91.

Hathaway, Oona A., and Scott J. Shapiro. *The Internationalists: How a Radical Plan to Outlaw War Remade the World*. New York: Simon and Schuster, 2017.

Lederach, John Paul. *Sustainable Reconciliation in Divided Societies*. Washington, DC: USIP, 1997.

———. *The Moral Imagination: The Art and Soul of Building Peace*. Reprint. Oxford: Oxford University Press, 2010.

Mac Ginty, Roger. "Indigenous Peace-Making Versus the Liberal Peace." *Cooperation and Conflict* 43, no. 2 (2008): 139–63.

Nobel, Alfred. "The Will." *Alfred Nobel's Will*, November 27, 1895. www.nobelprize.org/alfred_nobel/will/.

Piketty, Thomas. *Capital in the 21st Century*. Cambridge: Éditions du Seuil, Harvard University Press, 2014.

Quirk, Joel, and Darshan Vigneswaran. "The Construction of an Edifice: The Story of a First Great Debate." *Review of International Studies* (2005): 89–107.

Ramsbotham, Oliver. *Transforming Violent Conflict: Radical Disagreement, Dialogue and Survival*. London: Routledge, 2010.

———. "Is There a Theory of Radical Disagreement." *IJCER: International Journal of Computational Engineering Research* 1 (2013): 56.

Richmond, Oliver. *A Post-Liberal Peace*. London: Routledge, 2012.

Roosevelt, Franklin Delano. "D-Day Prayer." Franklin D. Roosevelt, Master Speech File, 1898–1945 | Franklin D. Roosevelt Presidential Library & Museum, June 6, 1944. www.fdrlibrary.marist.edu/archives/collections/franklin/index.php? p=collections/findingaid&id=582&q=d-day+prayer.

Rubenstein, Richard E. *Resolving Structural Conflicts: How Violent Systems Can Be Transformed*. London: Taylor & Francis, 2017.

Schmidt, Brian. *International Relations and the First Great Debate*. London: Routledge, 2013.

Simmons, Solon. *Root Narrative Theory and Conflict Resolution: Power, Justice and Values*. London: Routledge, 2020. doi:10.4324/9780367822712.

United Nations. "About the Sustainable Development Goals." *United Nations Sustainable Development* (blog), 2015. www.un.org/sustainabledevelopment/sustainable-development-goals/.

2 Lessons from disaster

History and the current crisis

Peter N. Stearns and Richard E. Rubenstein

The coronavirus pandemic and the economic upheaval caused by attempts to control it are unique in some ways, but they are not the first or the worst crises of this sort to beset human society. What can history tell us about how such events impact existing social conflicts and create new ones? What lessons can be learned about periods of recovery that follow, and the possibilities of resolving conflicts thought to be intractable? While biomedical crises are more apt to exacerbate existing conflicts than to initiate new ones, unique features of the current "multiple crisis" have the potential to generate movements of radical reform.

Beginning with the rapid spread of the coronavirus early in 2020, much of the world has been hit by a many-sided crisis, involving disease itself, massive economic dislocation, and popular protests against economic and racial inequality. The United States, beset as well by faltering national leadership and fundamental changes in demographic balance, has been particularly challenged. Each crisis raises questions about longer-term results, and their combination heightens a sense of urgency.

In modern societies, at least, crisis immediately calls forth a need for history: people want to know if similar disasters in the past provide any guidelines for evaluating the current issues and, perhaps, orchestrating solutions. Thus, as early as March 2020, historians were being called upon to help a wider public remember past plagues. Black Lives Matter demonstrations in May and June similarly galvanized recollections of 1968 and other past battles.

History matters, in response to crisis, for two reasons: first, it offers analogies from the past, which are immediately useful in providing benchmarks for the present. But second, it also contributes to the more difficult task of figuring out what might actually be new in a current challenge. Both services – analogy and evaluation of change – apply directly to the assessment of future prospects.

One final preliminary: in modern societies, crisis also provokes at least a brief conviction that "something must be done" to make sure not only that the current problem gets solved but that it never happens again. Many modern people believe deeply if vaguely in progress, in the ability for some combination of science and policy innovation to move us forward. This was another response that emerged early on in the pandemic, and it invites juxtaposition with the historical approach.

The plague pattern: analogies

We begin with the crisis that kicked everything off, the pandemic itself. Through the specific virus is new, the current epidemic quickly, and correctly, called forth reminders that the human species has encountered very much the same problem many times in the past. We know a lot about what happens during and after the challenge occurs. It is worth noting that, to date, the current pandemic is relatively mild: leave aside the Black Death of the fourteenth century, which swept away up to a third of populations in Europe and the Middle East; recurrent cholera epidemics less than two centuries ago routinely claimed upwards of a tenth of many urban clusters. Perhaps the first thing to note is the capacity of the human species, in sheer population terms, to recover surprisingly quickly from what might otherwise seem an overwhelming disaster.

But the other two central historical "lessons" about plague, deriving from past analogies, are markedly less encouraging. Plagues tend to reveal and exacerbate existing structural problems; and they rarely produce constructive change, aside from the demographic recovery.

A scholar and statesman in the eighteenth century lamented that "times of plague are always those in which the bestial and diabolical side of human nature gains the upper hand."[1] And while this might seem a bit harsh in the current crisis, some common symptoms do show through.

Thus, the rich always seek, and usually manage, to find ways to escape the worst ravages of plague, ways that are not available to ordinary people. Inequalities, already rampant, typically increase in the process. In a few particularly nasty cases, privileged groups even seek to spread the plague deliberately to more vulnerable populations; exchange of infected materials, even aggressive coughing, are one result. Plagues also provoke a brutal impulse to seek scapegoats. During the Black Death, Jews were systematically attacked. In the nineteenth century, Asians were a common target, again with sometimes violent results. Here too, effects of plague-enhanced hatreds can linger even after the crisis passes. Efforts to blame other countries, or to try to conceal death rates, are newer symptoms, but they began to crop up in the nineteenth and twentieth centuries.[2] It will take great and deliberate care to assure that these common responses do not distort our current crisis.

The second point, and partly the result of the further problems that epidemics usually generate, is the frequent lack of constructive, long-term results. Here, we need look no farther than the "Spanish" influenza crisis of 1918–19, which has, rightly, been much in the news of late. This was a deadly global event, markedly similar to our current challenge except in age-group vulnerability – yet very few measures to improve public health responses or to prevent further outbreaks were adopted. Australia did, to be sure, revamp its federal health organization. In the United States, an old habit, of using a single drinking glass for a school classroom, was abandoned for good. But that was about it. The crisis, overshadowed by the larger results of World War I, was quickly forgotten (and rarely recalled subsequently in the history books). In the United States, a few years later, it was as if upwards of 600,000 people had died to no purpose.[3]

There are, to be sure, exceptions to this bleak picture. Plagues can also bring out examples of human generosity. The Black Death, unusual in many respects, did ultimately generate pressures for social change, resulting in higher wages for laborers and a loosening of serfdom, as population loss forced better treatment of the workers who remained. But this is atypical: Plagues usually either have little durable effect or make things worse.

History lesson #1, then, in the current crisis: any expectation that a tragedy of this magnitude will *surely* generate positive reform is unrealistic. Improvement may result, but it will take deliberate and sustained effort.

The plague pattern: changes

Happily, in this case, there is a second history lesson: analogies are inexact, and there is reason to emphasize the ways in which the current crisis differs from past examples. There are two key points here, mutually related.

In the first place, most modern people, and certainly most Americans, are less inclined to accept the inevitability of plagues and other diseases than was the case just a century ago. Of course, we have had more recent epidemics, AIDS is the leading example, and threats like SARS, but there has been no experience of COVID-like rapid dissemination since 1919. This may mean that we are not only more shocked by the pandemic – and this is clearly true, compared to the influenza outbreak; news coverage has been far more extensive – but more insistent on major changes that will reduce the chance of recurrence.

This links to the second, and more basic point: modern people have become less tolerant of death, more insistent that responsible authorities do something about it. Signs of this began to emerge in the nineteenth century.

Already in 1838, after a severe typhus outbreak in Britain, reformer Edwin Chadwick managed to persuade a reluctant government (worried about infringing on "liberties") that sanitary conditions among the poor must be improved, not only for their sake but also for wider benefit.[4] Already in 1892, hesitant response by the government of Hamburg to a cholera episode caused the voters to remove it for incompetence[5] (just as, in 1920, American voters removed the national leadership that had overseen responses to the influenza, though in this case there were many factors involved).

Almost certainly, this kind of impatience has increased by the early twenty-first century. A considerable, though obviously not uniform, body of opinion has become intolerant of spikes in death rates – even, apparently, when old people are disproportionately involved. We also don't like situations in which lots of people die in public, rather than shielded by best efforts in a hospital – another response that was less uniform in 1919. Most obviously, many moderns have greatly extended both a belief in "science" and an insistence that science come up with rapid remedies.

Whether these raised expectations will overmaster the limitations suggested by historical analogies is, of course, unclear. We cannot even be sure that impatience with fumbling responses will topple existing governments, though current public opinion polls suggest some possibilities. At the least, we are not trapped by analogy: those seeking change can work to heighten the new impatience about death, to seek to address some of the deep, underlying problems the pandemic has revealed.

One other point deserves mention. The global context in which the pandemic has unfolded is also unusual. Epidemics have always, of course, involved international contacts – the Black Death spread from China to the Middle East to Europe; cholera usually reached Europe from India and then on to the Americas. Responses to epidemics have also had global repercussions: quarantines have affected trade and migration flows at least since the fourteenth century. But the current crisis, involving tensions around existing global institutions like the World Health Organization and amid the mounting competition between the United States and China, may have wider, and less predictable, implications. The result could exacerbate hostilities or provide another motive for more constructive reform.

The confluence of crises

By late spring 2020, it was becoming obvious that the pandemic was hardly the only concern. Disruption of trade and collapse of employment inevitably led to comparisons with the Great Recession and the Depression of the 1930s. Then, on top of this came a wave of civil rights protests that, again, had its own historical precedents.

Each strand invites its own mixture of analogy and change analysis, applying both to the nature of the crisis and to the adequacy of prior response. We do know, for example, some of the measures that can be taken to recover from a downward spiral – though the record, both in the 1930s and in 2008–9, suggests that Western societies, at least, are often too timid, extending hardship far longer than necessary. This is also a good time to assess the responses to the earlier civil rights movement, which were not negligible, but which demonstrably fell way short of the mark, in areas such as police behavior and imprisonment. We can also usefully compare public response, where at least in the short run, attitudes toward racial injustice seem to be shifting rapidly compared to the divisions of the late 1960s.

But what is arguably most remarkable, from the standpoint of historical analogy, is how rare it is to confront three crises of this magnitude – disease, economic collapse, civil rights surge – simultaneously. The three strands obviously interrelate – racial imbalance in pandemic incidence feeds response to police brutality, and all three crises highlight structural economic inequalities, all of course in the context of a changing global balance of power. Under circumstances this unusual, one's use of historical analogy must be cautious, especially considering that it is not yet clear how deep and long the economic downturn will be, or how rapid and complete a recovery can be expected. Even so, history offers some tantalizing suggestions.

First, multiple crises even more disastrous than the current crop have occurred in some situations that produced revolutions or counter-revolutions. The Russian Revolution of 1917 took place on the heels of World War I, which ravaged the economy and virtually destroyed the Russian Army as an effective fighting force. The Nazi counter-revolution of 1933 was the product of multiple crises including Germany's defeat in the World War I, punitive measures by the Allies, and the Great Depression, which struck Germany earlier and more fiercely than it did other nations. Clearly, this does *not* mean that revolutionary changes of this sort are in the offing for nations now afflicted by the coronavirus and economic recession. But there is evidence that people undergoing multiple crises are inclined to view the source of their problems as a defective *system* rather than simply poor leadership or some other temporary condition.

This was the case, for example, during the 1930s Depression, when a large coalition of activist groups supporting President Franklin D, Roosevelt's New Deal pushed him to change the old system by creating a welfare state, undertaking massive infrastructure reforms, and guaranteeing the rights of labor unions. A revolution did not take place in the United States, but systemic thinking helped generate substantial reforms. It is certainly possible, although by no means inevitable, that the sort of systemic criticism that already characterizes the thinking of activists in groups like Black Lives

Matter will become more marked among other aggrieved groups, such as workers and lower-level professionals.

Second, in an age in which conservative nationalism of a "populist" sort has become an important movement around the globe, it is quite possible that multiple crises will produce a more pronounced shift to the right. We cannot foresee how people in diverse societies will choose to exercise their political power, but we can say that the political decisions to be made at times like this are particularly fraught, since these battles tend not to be between moderates of various stripes but rather between (relative) extremists. By the time this book appears, the U.S. presidential election of 2020 will be history, but it is as good an example of any of the high stakes political decisions that may be made in eras of multiple crisis.

Finally, where multiple crises are long-lived and are followed by lengthy, halting, and uneven periods of recovery (as during the Great Depression), an alteration of political psychology can generate sustained movements for radical reform. From the time of the "Anarchist Prince," Peter Kropotkin, to the work of scholars like Ted Robert Gurr and Charles Tilly, analysts have noted that a period of recovery that raises and intensifies popular expectations for further improvement is more likely to produce mass movements for change than a straight downward spiral. In this regard, it is also worth remembering that the three interrelated crises we have been discussing could well turn out to be the forerunners of additional crises, including environmental disasters related to climate change, new economic challenges, and an unpredictable global military environment.

To summarize: historical analogies stimulate speculation by calling attention both to similar past events and to unique aspects of the present. Predicting the likely outcome of an era of multiple crises is no simpler a matter than predicting the future of any other era, but one thing seems fairly clear: the post-coronavirus world is not likely to return easily to some pre-coronavirus state of "normalcy." Confidence in public institutions has been deeply shaken. Systemic inequalities and incapacities have been dramatically exposed. Certain vulnerable social groups are already redefining their relationships with other groups and the State. How time-consuming and difficult the post-corona recovery will be is impossible to say at this point, but we would not be surprised, years from now, to see the 2020s described as a decade of intense and fateful turmoil.

Here, the citizen can only hope for a combination of popular pressure and responsive leadership to generate the range of dramatic changes that an extraordinary mixture seems to call for—a combination that has not clearly emerged, in Western societies, since at least the later 1940s. And here the historian (who also happens to be advanced in years) must simply wonder at

the magnitude of the challenge involved, compared to available precedent –
wonder, and perhaps hope.

Notes

1 Barthold Niebuhr (1816), quoted in Samuel Cohn, *Epidemics: Hate and Compassion from the Plague of Athens to AIDS* (Oxford: Oxford University Press, 2019).
2 Cohn, *Epidemics*.
3 John Barry, *The Great Influenza: The Epic Story of the Deadliest Plague in History* (New York: Viking Press, 2004).
4 Christopher Hamlin, *Public Health and Social Justice in the Age of Chadwick: Britain, 1800–1854* (New York: Cambridge University Press, 1998).
5 Richard Evan, *Death in Hamburg: Society and Politics in the Cholera Years* (New York: Penguin Books, 2005).

3   From the frying pan to the fire

Environmental crises and their implications for conflict resolution

Michael Shank

The current pandemic and its socio-economic effects can be considered the opening salvo in a series of potential crises caused by human activities that are redefining the relations between humankind and the natural environment. This essay describes the threats most likely to produce escalated social conflicts in the immediate and medium-term future. Considering the difficulties of changing well-entrenched complex systems, what can be done to alter the conditions producing biomedical crises, climatic disasters, and destructive industrial practices? The author suggests how these challenges are likely to alter methods of conflict mitigation and resolution, outlining new methods that might prove effective under post-pandemic conditions.

Introduction

Two environmentally rooted crises – the planetary crisis and the current pandemic – deserve the conflict field's attention with preventive, not only responsive, approaches. Conflicts emerging from these crises, such as climate refugee claims, resource wars, unequal socio-economic impacts from COVID-19, and disputes over health mandates, merit response. But prevention is paramount when transforming systems that exploit natural and human capital. The systems that caused the climate crisis and coronavirus rely on resource extraction, fossil fuels, factory farming, deforestation, and destruction of natural habitat. They intersect on impacts – e.g., higher COVID-19 death rates are linked with air pollution (Friedman 2020)[1] – and they will continue to instigate conflict until production and consumption of energy and food are sustainably managed. In response, this chapter presents pathways for the conflict community to assist in transforming these conflict-promoting systems. A first step is to narratively position them as structurally violent; a second step is to widen the field and build a multidisciplinary practice in order to dismantle these systems and rebuild regenerative alternatives.

Structurally violent systems

The conflict field is ever-evolving (Kriesberg 2009, 15)[2] and exploring new frontiers in systems and behavior change. Using Johan Galtung's work on structural violence, this chapter encourages the field to go further. In identifying the economic, political, or cultural structures that prevent the fulfillment of the basic human needs, Galtung also encouraged the field to focus on "social injustice" (Galtung 1969, 171),[3] which is germane to this chapter since energy and food systems have disproportionately negative consequences for, and human need-limiting impacts on, low-income communities and communities of color:

> *Fossil fuel facilities* adversely impact low-income communities (Israel 2012)[4] and communities of color (NAACP 2014)[5] by locating air-, water- and land-polluting oil, coal, and gas plants within these communities, exposing them to health-deteriorating toxins and contaminants.
>
> *Factory farm facilities*, which produce the majority of cow, pork, and poultry products in the United States and the majority of pork and poultry products globally (Harvey et al 2017),[6] are responsible for air, water and land pollution in low-income communities and communities of color (Nicole 2013).[7] Factory farms are also reliant on immigrant and undocumented labor (Spangher 2014)[8] and culpable for pandemics that have disproportionate health impacts on communities of color (Godoy 2020).[9]

The conflict community has an opportunity to utilize Galtung's structural violence framing, and social justice narratives, to address both need-limiting systems. As Richard E. Rubenstein noted in his book *Resolving Structural Conflicts* (Rubenstein 2017, 2),[10] it is the conflict field's job is to discover what these arrangements are, which cause violent conflict, and transform them.

By exploring the climate crisis and coronavirus through structural violence lenses, and examining how these systems prevent fulfillment of basic human needs, the field can begin to articulate how fossil fuels responsible for the current climate crisis (IPCC 2013),[11] and animal farming, deforestation and destruction of natural habitat, which produced COVID-19 and the majority of recent pandemics (Dalton 2020),[12] can be addressed by the conflict community.

Climate and conflict

The climate crisis is generating ample conflict. Global heating is creating deadly heat waves, permanent droughts, recurring wildfires, and more torrential storms, displacing millions of people and increasing armed conflict up to 20% (Mach, Kraan, and Adger 2019, 194).[13] Aided by rising sea levels, it is estimated to displace 1 billion people by 2050 (Kamal 2017).[14] It is already destroying countless homes, mobilizing a burgeoning climate refugee population, and escalating competition over scarce resources. There are nearly 1,000 global conflicts, to date, with water as the root cause (World Water, n.d.),[15] and the "causal and substantive linkages . . . between food security and violent conflict, spanning the individual, local, regional, country and global levels" are well-documented by the Food and Agricultural Organization (Martin-Shields and Stojetz, 2018, 23).[16]

There is ample work *resolving* these climate conflicts, whether in territorial disputes over water resources, conflicts over food scarcity, or physical violence experienced by climate refugees. Instead of a conflict *response*, however, this section focuses on the need for *preventive* practice in transforming fossil-fueled systems.

Fossil fuels, the systems they energize, and the behaviors they enable, are structurally violent in three primary ways. First, exploitative oil, coal, and gas extraction practices pollute resource-adjacent communities' air, water, and land. Second, distribution systems for these fuels are often located within under-resourced communities, similarly polluting their air, water, and land. And third, the burning of oil, coal, and gas further pollutes, causing premature death in seven million people annually (WHO 2014).[17] In response, the conflict field has an opportunity to pioneer a multidisciplinary practice, in coordination with environmental, racial, and justice fields, in co-creating just, nonviolent alternatives.

Many of these fossil-fueled systems are located near urban areas since cities are hubs for fuel transport and represent the majority of the world's energy use. (In response, cities like Portland, Oregon, and New York City are banning new fossil fuel infrastructure.) Embedding conflict practitioners within a city's environmental practice – and its racial and social justice work, which has been reinvigorated given recent global protests – and training conflict practitioners to serve as co-designers of the urban experience, and that which fuels it, could help prevent conflict across the fuel supply chain. Global cities are transforming their energy systems more aggressively than many large national polluters, which is why the ground for collaboration among urban practitioners is particularly fertile.

Cities are also reconfiguring in response to COVID-19. Environmental staff are being seconded to social services, and there is new cross-departmental coordination that invites a rethink of how policymakers can best serve society in a multidisciplinary, versus siloed, way. Since greenhouse gas emissions must be halved by 2030 to prevent irreversible climate chaos (Harvey 2019),[18] this kind of outside-the-box thinking is necessary.

It is time to complement conflict *response* – e.g., resolving resource wars, managing resource scarcity, and transforming climate refugee relationships – with new investments in conflict *prevention* and the design of structurally nonviolent systems. By partnering with environmental, racial and social justice practitioners, operating across the urban and academic space, the conflict field demonstrates its ability to remain agile amid emerging conflicts and apply itself to sociology in new ways.

The narrative moment for questioning the exploitative capitalism economy on which fossil fuel systems depend is now; policymaker conversations abound regarding the "end of capitalism." Furthermore, regenerative systems and solutions, referenced below, are becoming mainstream. These are all good signs for an academic rethink of the system. The first step now is to position, and structure the way the field understands, key components of this system as "structurally violent."

COVID-19 and conflict

Food systems vary little from energy systems: they are as exploitative and extractive, whether in informal slaughterhouses in Wuhan, China, or formal ones in Waco, Texas. The practice of crowding animals into unsanitary, unsafe conditions for sale and slaughter is responsible for the majority of pandemics in recent history, including COVID-19 (Foer and Gross 2020).[19] Most animal product consumed globally is raised in factory-farmed, pathogen-friendly environments, where thousands of animals are packed into small spaces to maximize efficiency. This system is dependent on widespread deforestation and habitat destruction, which also contributed to COVID-19 (Einhorn 2020).[20]

In redesigning this system, the conflict community has a role. Food behaviors are perceived as personal or cultural and thus, potentially, intractable. (Fossil fuels can be personal when impacting food, fashion and family planning, but the bigger carbon contributors – i.e. buildings, transportation, and waste – are not as burdened by cultural constrictions.) Transitioning from industrial animal agricultural requires a sea change in food production and consumption and a commitment to making food regeneratively. Conversations about food require the kind of intervention that the conflict field is trained to handle. Culture-and-conflict studies are well-developed and need to expand to include food systems.

Behavioral barriers are not insignificant. Heavily subsidized animal agriculture makes factory-farmed meat cheaper for mass consumption (Shapiro 2016),[21] and meat is associated with economic prosperity (Bereżnicka and Pawlonka 2018, 18–19)[22] and identity – e.g., meat is very "American" (Ziegelman 2020).[23] Positioning patriotic identities around plant-based diets, then, which have a substantially lower carbon footprint, requires new narratives. When Canadian Prime Minister Justin Trudeau recently directed $100 million to the plant-based protein industry, he boasted that by "using 100 percent Canadian inputs, it will also support farmers" and that "standing up for hard-working farmers, creating good jobs, [and] setting up Canada for success on the world stage" are things Canada will always get behind (Global News 2020).[24] This patriotic repositioning and jobs-based framing make alternative plant-based identities viable.

Disarming this system yields significant benefits by avoiding premature deaths – from COVID-19 and future pandemics – and preventing exploitative and extractive practices. While conflict *responses* to COVID-19-related disputes – e.g., labor disputes by undocumented factory farm workers (Grabel 2017),[25] violent disputes over COVID-19 mask-wearing (Hutchinson 2020),[26] or environmental disputes over factory farming's polluting practices in low-income communities of color (EWG 2016)[27] – are necessary. But they are responses, and, while helpful in reducing conflict, may fail to transform the system.

Preventive practice proposes a buildout in the conflict field that embraces food policy, specifically the field of regenerative agriculture (which, discussed below, is helpful in reducing climate-crisis-causing carbon emissions). By engaging sectors that deal with food systems decision-making within international institutions (e.g., Food and Agriculture Organization),[28] national governments (e.g., departments and ministries of food and agriculture), and the private sector, the redesign of food systems can be influenced through a conflict lens. This calls for a recognition by the field of food's role in creating conflict, and, subsequently, partnerships across multiple disciplines to ensure the field's foothold in this space going forward.

From restorative to regenerative

There is another way to change these systems: foster behavior changes as a way of forcing systems change, since these industries depend on consumer demand. Modeling *restorative* justice's role in transforming the criminal justice system, the conflict field could add to its practice the study of *regenerative* economics (Fath et al 2019),[29] in which goods and services contribute to well-being rather than undermining it, and *regenerative* agriculture (LaCanne and Lundgren 2018),[30] which focuses on rehabilitative approaches that enhance ecosystems rather than eroding them. Both could reorient energy and food systems, prevent conflict emergence, and grow the field.

Going further, similar to how restorative justice brings together victims and offenders to reconcile wrongs (Zehr 2002),[31] the conflict community could convene stakeholders to transform fossil-fueled and factory-farmed systems. With fossil fuels, the conflict field could convene offenders (individuals with the heaviest carbon footprints) and victims (those exposed to pollutants and hit hardest by climate impacts) to address grievances and reconcile wrongs. These conversations do occur, but not in a restorative way, at international climate talks (Mathiesen 2013),[32] where conflicts emerge over whether industrialized nations should or should not pay for their historical responsibility in creating climate change and redress wrongs to frontline communities.

The conflict field could also convene offenders in the industrial animal food system (individual consumers of factory-farmed meat) and its victims (populations impacted by deforestation, immigrant workers in factory farms, and low-income communities of color adjacent to factory farms) to understand the impact of their consumption. These relational approaches – allowing offenders to understand the consequences of their actions – may prove effective in transforming consumer demand. While these approaches are primarily utilized within systems causing direct physical violence, the potential to use them within structurally violent systems should also be explored.

Lastly, it is important to note that a shift from exploitative to regenerative practices will not happen immediately, but COVID-19 is increasing the feasibility of system-wide and behavioral shifts. There are moves across all levels of government to boost the *health, resilience, safety* and *security* of economic and agricultural systems, which are helpful narratives and frames when marketing to basic human needs.

All of this signals a potential systems and behavioral shift toward economic and agricultural models that are smaller in scope, less industrial in scale, more responsive to negative externalities, and, potentially, more regenerative in practice. Add to this wave of reform, the social and racial justice awareness, narrative, and protest that can be harnessed to address the negative impacts from fossil fuel and factory farm industries on under-resourced and under-represented communities. The conflict field can thus further motivate these shifts by engaging in the multidisciplinary partnerships and narrative framing suggested in this chapter.

Conclusion

As emissions rise and biodiversity rapidly disappears, planetary crises and pandemics become more prevalent and conflicts more pervasive. The conflict field should seize this transitional moment to bring on board the academic and policy partnerships necessary to engage in the transformation of fossil-fueled and factory-farmed systems and the behaviors that support

them. By treating the climate crisis and coronavirus in preventive, not only
responsive, ways, the conflict field influences a transformational moment
and ensures the field remains resilient amid emerging environmental crises.
Now is the time to rethink the conflict scope and map new areas of interest,
including energy and food systems, building the necessary narratives and
multidisciplinary infrastructure to address these structurally violent systems.

Notes

1 Lisa Friedman, "New Research Links Air Pollution to Higher Coronavirus
  Death Rates," *New York Times*, April 7, 2020, www.nytimes.com/2020/04/07/
  climate/air-pollution-coronavirus-covid.html.
2 Louis Kriesberg, "Evolution of Conflict Resolution," in *The Sage Handbook of
  Conflict Resolution*, ed. Jacob Bercovitch, Victor Kremenyuk, and I. William
  Zartman, 15–32. (Thousand Oaks, CA: Sage, 2009).
3 Johan Galtung, "Violence, Peace and Peace Research," *Journal of Peace
  Research* 6, no. 3 (1969): 167–91.
4 Brett Israel, "Coal Plants Smother Communities of Color," *Scientific American*,
  November 16, 2012, www.scientificamerican.com/article/coal-plants-smother-
  communities-of-color/.
5 National Association for the Advancement of Colored People, "Just Energy
  Policies: Reducing Pollution and Creating Jobs," 2014, accessed June 26, 2020.
6 Fiona Harvey, Andrew Wasley, Madlen Davies, and David Child, "Rise of Mega
  Farms: How the US Model of Intensive Farming Is Invading the World," *The
  Guardian*, July 18, 2017, www.theguardian.com/environment/2017/jul/18/rise-
  of-mega-farms-how-the-us-model-of-intensive-farming-is-invading-the-world.
7 Wendee Nicole, "CAFOs and Environmental Justice: The Case of North
  Carolina," *Environmental Health Perspectives* 121, no. 6 (2013): A182–89,
  doi:10.1289/ehp.121-a182.
8 Lucas Spangher, "The Overlooked Plight of Factory Farm Workers," *Huffing-
  ton Post*, August 18, 2014, www.huffpost.com/entry/plight-of-factory-farm-
  workers_b_5662261; NAACP, 2014, www.naacp.org/wp-content/uploads/2014/
  03/Just-Energy-Policies-Compendium-EXECUTIVE-SUMMARY_NAACP.
  pdf.
9 Maria Godoy, "What Do Coronavirus Racial Disparities Look Like State By State?"
  NPR, May 30, 2020, www.npr.org/sections/health-shots/2020/05/30/865413079/
  what-do-coronavirus-racial-disparities-look-like-state-by-state.
10 Rubenstein, *Resolving Structural Conflicts*.
11 IPCC, *Climate Change 2013: The Physical Science Basis* (Cambridge and New
   York: Cambridge University Press, 2013), p. 1535, accessed June 29, 2020,
   www.ipcc.ch/report/ar5/wg1/.
12 Jane Dalton, "Coronavirus: Industrial Animal Farming Has Caused Most New
   Infectious Diseases and Risks More Pandemics, Experts Warn," *The Independent*,
   May 8, 2020, www.independent.co.uk/environment/coronavirus-meat-animal-
   farming-pandemic-disease-wet-markets-a9505626.html.
13 Katharine J. Mach, Caroline M. Kraan, W. Neil Adger et al., "Climate as a Risk
   Factor for Armed Conflict," *Nature* 571 (2019): 193–97, https://doi.org/10.1038/
   s41586-019-1300-6.

14 Baher Kamal, "Climate Migrants Might Reach One Billion by 2050," *Inter Press Service*, August 21, 2017, www.ipsnews.net/2017/08/climate-migrants-might-reach-one-billion-by-2050/.

15 World Water, "Water Conflict Chronology," n.d., accessed June 26, 2020, www.worldwater.org/conflict/list/.

16 Charles P. Martin-Shields and Wolfgang Stojetz, "Food Security and Conflict: Empirical Challenges and Future Opportunities for Research and Policy Making on Food Security and Conflict," in *FAO Agricultural Development Economics Working Paper 18–04* (Rome: FAO, 2018), Licence: CC BY-NC-SA 3.0 IGO.

17 World Health Organization, "7 Million Premature Deaths Annually Linked to Air Pollution," 2014, accessed June 26, 2020, www.who.int/mediacentre/news/releases/2014/air-pollution/en/.

18 Fiona Harvey, "Scientists Set Out How to Halve Greenhouse Gas Emissions by 2030," *The Guardian*, September 19, 2019, www.theguardian.com/environment/2019/sep/19/power-halve-greenhouse-gas-emissions-2030-climate-scientists.

19 Jonathan S. Foer and Aaron S. Gross, "We Have to Wake Up: Factory Farms Are Breeding Grounds for Pandemics," *The Guardian*, April 20, 2020, www.theguardian.com/commentisfree/2020/apr/20/factory-farms-pandemic-risk-covid-animal-human-health.

20 Catrin Einhorn, "Animal Viruses Are Jumping to Humans: Forest Loss Makes It Easier," *New York Times*, April 9, 2020, www.nytimes.com/2020/04/09/climate/animals-humans-virus-covid.html.

21 Paul Shapiro, "The Elephant-Sized Subsidy in the Race," *National Review*, February 17, 2016, www.nationalreview.com/2016/02/end-farm-subsidies-now/.

22 Joanna Bereżnicka and Tomasz Pawlonka, "Meat Consumption as an Indicator of Economic Well-Being," *Acta Scientiarum Polonorum Oeconomia* 17, no. 2 (2018): 17–26, doi:10.22630/ASPE.2018.17.2.17.

23 Jane Ziegelman, "America's Obsession with Cheap Meat," *New York Times*, May 15, 2020, www.nytimes.com/2020/05/15/opinion/coronavirus-meat-beef.html.

24 Global News, "Winnipeg Plant Gets $100M in Federal Financing to Pull Protein from Peas, Canola," *Global News*, June 22, 2020, https://globalnews.ca/news/7093654/winnipeg-plant-gets-100m-in-federal-financing-to-pull-protein-from-peas-canola/.

25 Michael Grabel, "Exploitation and Abuse at the Chicken Plant," *New Yorker*, May 1, 2017, www.newyorker.com/magazine/2017/05/08/exploitation-and-abuse-at-the-chicken-plant.

26 Bill Hutchinson, " 'Incomprehensible': Confrontations Over Masks Erupt Amid COVID-19 Crisis," *ABC News*, May 7, 2020, https://abcnews.go.com/US/incomprehensible-confrontations-masks-erupt-amid-COVID-19-crisis/story?id=70494577.

27 Environmental Working Group, "Landmark Report Maps Feces-Laden Hog and Chicken Operations in North Carolina," 2016, accessed June 26, 2020, www.ewg.org/research/exposing-fields-filth.

28 "Food Systems," *Civil Eats*, May 18, 2020, https://civileats.com/2020/05/18/in-the-face-of-COVID-19-state-legislators-push-for-federal-support-of-local-food-systems/.

29 Brian D. Fath, and Daniel A. Fiscus, Sally J. Goerner, Anamaria Berea, and Robert E. Ulanowicz, "Measuring Regenerative Economics: 10 Principles and

Measures Undergirding Systemic Economic Health," *Global Transitions* 1 (2019): 15–27, doi:10.1016/j.glt.2019.02.002.

30 Claire LaCanne and Jonathan Lundgren, "Regenerative Agriculture: Merging Farming and Natural Resource Conservation Profitably," *PeerJ* 6 (2018): e4428, doi:10.7717/peerj.4428.

31 Howard Zehr, *The Little Book of Restorative Justice* (Intercourse, PA: Good Books, 2002).

32 Karl Mathiesen, "Climate Talks: Should Rich Countries Pay for Damage Caused by Global Warming?" *The Guardian*, November 20, 2013, www.theguardian.com/environment/2013/nov/20/climate-talks-rich-countries-pay-damage-global-warming.

Part II

Global political conflicts after the pandemic

4 Pandemics, globalization, and contentious politics

Agnieszka Paczynska and Terrence Lyons

The immediate effects of the pandemic on globalization are ambiguous; the crisis stimulates reversals of globalization while also demonstrating its inescapability. What, then, of the wave of protests around the globe that made 2019 one of the most active protest years in recent memory? The current crisis may lead to a shift in tactics and at least a temporary advantage for authoritarian regimes. Nevertheless, comparative examples suggest that contentious politics and social movements will adjust to the new context and develop new tactics to pursue their demands for social justice.

Processes of globalization that once seemed relentless faced daunting challenges in the 2010s. Trade wars and neo-mercantilist policies, xenophobic reactions to migration, and increased nationalism in the United States and parts of Europe threatened to slow if not reverse decades of increasing interconnectedness and interdependence. The global spread of the coronavirus in 2020, however, reflected both the continued salience of globalization and its greatest challenge. On the one hand, international travel facilitated the virus' swift spread and the search for a vaccine became a matter of global interdependent research and competition. But, on the other hand, the pandemic led to the shuttering of international borders, the near collapse of cultural and educational exchanges, an economic recession that reduced global trade, and attacks on key institutions at the center of global health policies such as the World Health Organization.

This chapter will focus on how globalization as manifested in the COVID-19 pandemic shaped patterns of contentious politics around the world. The concept of contentious politics, initially coined by Charles Tilly and his colleagues, has developed into an interdisciplinary subfield that has expanded beyond its initial concerns with social movements to consider a wider set of conflictual phenomena, from street protests and patterns of state repression to civil wars and revolutions.[1] The contentious politics approach emphasizes relational mechanisms, thereby allowing scholars to study movements and institutional politics interactively. Key processes are the competing and often transgressive forms of claim-making where one party making claims is the government. These processes are inherently about power but often unfold outside of formal political institutions.

This orientation provides a framework for research that highlights the transitions and relationships between different forms of contention and encourages the investigation of how one form of contention, say a civil war, emerges from an earlier form of contention, such as a nonviolent social movement. The approach separates the nature of the claim and the social mobilization from the "repertoire of contention," that is, the tactics deployed. It assumes that social change and power shifts often emerge endogenously from struggles among parties without assuming that dialogue or problem-solving are the only means to advance justice. These struggles between states and social groups are now taking new urgency and adopting new repertoires as the COVID-19 pandemic lays bare and further deepens structural inequalities that fueled the Fall 2019 global wave of protests.

Globalization and both violent and nonviolent forms of contentious politics are interlinked. Civil wars, for example, have become increasingly transnational as global trade and investment as well as the circulation of people and ideas intensified, providing new ways to finance armed conflict and to engage with global actors to support an often distant cause.[2] Social movements and nonviolent forms of contentious politics likewise have been shaped by globalization and accompanying shifts in technology as activists could more easily connect with global advocacy organizations as well as each other and share strategies, tactics, and resources. For instance, members of *Otpor* (Resistance), the Serb nonviolent movement that helped topple the regime of Slobodan Milosevic in 2000, trained activists from the Middle East in the run-up to the Arab uprisings in 2010.[3] It is notable that waves of contentious politics are often geographically centered, as with the 1989 protests in East and Central Europe and the Arab Uprisings of 2010–2011, but not in the case in street protests of 2019.[4] New technologies, including the Internet, mobile phones, and social media, have also facilitated the diffusion of nonviolent strategies and strengthened transnational networks among activists. At the same time, repressive states have capitalized on technology to more effectively monitor and suppress opposition.

Contentious politics during a time of pandemic

In 2019, the world saw an extraordinary wave of street protests that included massive demonstrations in Hong Kong, Sudan, Lebanon, Algeria, France, Chile, and Iran, among many others. Some dubbed 2019 the "year of street protests." Contentious politics contributed to the change of political leadership in Iraq, Lebanon, Sudan, Bolivia and important political concessions in Chile, Hong Kong, and other cases. Most demonstrations began and remained nonviolent, but harsh repression in Iraq and Iran led to the killing of hundreds of protestors. While the sources of grievance and the goals of those engaging in different episodes of protest varied and reflected local contexts, many if not most were sparked by economic hardships, the removal of subsidies for basic goods, and frustrations with deepening social inequalities and pervasive corruption. A significant number had feminist agendas at their core, as the #MeToo movement diffused and went global. Issues of social justice and a general rage against what many young people saw as dysfunctional traditional political classes animated many of these actions. Protests tended to focus on institutions that sustained inequalities and drew on shared symbolic imagery, such as the global adoption of the creepy grin of the Joker mask inspired by the 2019 film or the Chilean feminist protest chant "the rapist is you" which quickly spread to other countries.[5]

Protests were often led by young people mobilized through social networks rather than formal organizations. Many followed patterns seen in Tahrir Square in Cairo, Maidan Square in Kiev, and Gezi Park in Istanbul and occupied key symbolic places. To show commitment, many remained mobilized for months, as in Hong Kong, France, and Algeria. The ability to return large numbers of supporters onto the streets and into public spaces week in and week out represented a key signal of levels of support, unity, commitment, and power to shape policy outcomes. These movements typically demonstrated considerable social media sophistication. Iconic images of Alaa Salah, a Sudanese woman singing in her *thoub* from the roof of a car during a sit-in around army headquarters, or protestors in Hong Kong with umbrellas blocking tear gas, or graffiti in Beirut and Santiago underlined the importance of the visual. "Viral" images shaped contentious politics before the coronavirus.

The COVID-19 pandemic exacerbated existing tensions and created new ones, thereby heightening the grievances around which protestors already had mobilized. State leaders, often seen as corrupt and ineffectual, demonstrated their inability or unwillingness to respond to the threat. Communities previously marginalized were impoverished further as economies stalled. Lebanon and Sudan in particular neared economic collapse. At the same time, however, COVID-19 at first stifled this wave of demands for change, as governments used the opportunities afforded by the pandemic to impose new controls over their populations, to postpone elections, shrink political space, and ban mass meetings. Millions of activists across the globe left the streets and hunkered down at home following lockdown and shelter-at-home orders. National elections in Ethiopia and Bolivia and a referendum to change Chile's constitution, among many other polls, were postponed. China used the pandemic as the opportunity to crack down on protest in Hong Kong. An Indian activist reflecting on new restrictions on opposition gatherings stated "this government is lucky."[6]

This, of course, is not the first time that the world has grappled with pandemics. Over the past centuries, pandemics have regularly swept across continents. While these epidemics and pandemics have delivered death and devastation, they also sometimes ushered in social and political change. Historians see the Plague of Cyprian as hastening the collapse of the Roman Empire, Black Death contributed to the downfall of feudalism in Europe and the devastation wrought by the Spanish flu ushered in changes in the way many states constructed their public health systems later in the century.[7] At the same time, pandemics historically exposed and amplified structural inequalities in societies, thereby fueling grievances. Protests and revolts ignited by the Black Death included the 1381 peasant revolt in England and the Spanish flu strengthened the anti-colonial movement in India. The yellow fever in Philadelphia led to the publication of a pamphlet by two African American pastors, who pushed against racist narratives circulating in the city during the epidemic and called for abolition of slavery. We see a similar pattern emerge during the contemporary COVID-19 pandemic of 2020.

Contentious politics as a rule evolves with new techniques of mass mobilization being challenged by new forms of repression, leading to innovations by those demanding change. As has long been seen in the case of comparative studies of contentious politics, innovative social movements generate changes in government responses, which in turn result in new forms of creative political engagement. The pandemic of 2020 illustrates these larger recursive processes in particularly dramatic forms.

Innovation and contentious politics

The restrictions of the COVID-19 pandemic transformed the opportunities for social movements to pursue their goals through the mass street protests and occupations that characterized 2019.[8] While this particular genre initially lost momentum, the underlying connections and commitments to social justice remained undiminished. In many places, including Tunisia, Algeria, and Lebanon, social movement networks transformed from organizing protests to providing support for marginalized communities impoverished and devastated by both the virus and the collapse of the economy. In Hong Kong, activists turned workshops that had been used to make props for streets demonstrations into facilities to make and distribute hand sanitizer, providing a new focus to keep networks active and to underline the government's fecklessness. In Brazil, *Coletivo Rapo Reto* shifted from reporting on police abuses in Rio de Janeiro to monitoring fake news about the virus.

Social networks, particularly those based on social media, have repurposed themselves into mutual aid initiatives, matching volunteers with actions to respond to the virus and those it infects. In Algeria and Lebanon, the protest movements increasingly focused on providing food and medical supplies to neighborhoods most devastated by the pandemic.[9] The capacities and commitments of groups demanding political change remained while the specific targets of government failure shifted.

In other cases, however, protests movements responded with new and innovative contentious actions that reduced the dangers from large and concentrated crowds but retained the focus and the ability to signal the movement's size, commitment, and political power. In a number of places, protestors used social media to remain active in the public sphere. In northern Europe, climate strike activists shifted to online meetings and public advocacy that targeted specific government institutions. In Poland, protestors organized car parades and covered windows and balconies with the slogan *Przełóźmy Wybory* (postpone the election), which then were edited and distributed on social media as a way to signal the continued determination of the opposition movement.[10] In others, particularly in Spain and South America, street protests shifted to balconies and the banging of pots and pans – known as *cacerolazo* – replaced speeches and chants. *Coordinadora 8M*, a Chilean feminist advocacy group, projected images of crowds onto walls and activists organized weekly cacerolazo demanding the release of protestors from prison.[11] In yet other cases, notably Lebanon, parades on foot were replaced by car rallies, where streets could be occupied by protestors honking horns and waving flags out of sunroofs while retaining physical distance.[12] In Belarus, where public displays of opposition to president Lukashenko have in the past been swiftly repressed, the pandemic made protests possible, as fear of reprisals declined with anonymity provided by the previously banned face masks.[13] Following what was seen as a rigged presidential election, mass protests escalated in August.

Finally, in spite of COVID-19, mass protests remain a key instrument in movements to advance social justice. Sparked by the wide distribution of video showing the chilling killing of George Perry Floyd Jr. by police in Minneapolis, a wave of streets protests erupted across the United States. As was the pattern in the 2019 protests around the world, these were overwhelmingly nonviolent and relied upon social media and informal forms of organization to bring large crowds, particularly into symbolic spaces such as the area where Floyd was killed, Lafayette Park in Washington DC, and Centennial Park in Atlanta, in front of statues of Confederate Army soldiers in Richmond and Chapel Hill, as well as in front of city halls and court houses in small towns. Even under the restrictions of the pandemic, sports teams and athletes went on strike to demand action against structural racism. Large solidarity protests were organized in Europe and elsewhere, demonstrating the power of globalized media and the rapid spread of ideas and symbols. Statues often served as a focal point for demonstrations. In Oxford, protestors demanded the removal of a statue of Cecil Rhodes, in Bristol a statue of seventeenth-century slave trader Edward Colston was dragged into the city's harbor, and in Belgium, protestors defaced and demanded the removal of a statue of King Leopold II.

The demand for dignity resonated globally. In India, events in the United States, bolstered by statements of support from major Bollywood stars, sparked a discussion of police brutality against India's poor and marginalized minorities. Black Lives Matter protests provided a vocabulary and repertoire of contention that bolstered movements in the United Kingdom and France to re-examine their own imperial histories and racialized hierarchies. Protestors in Ethiopia donned T-shirts that said "Oromo Lives Matter." Korean pop stars BTS sent \$1 million to Black Lives Matter and used their considerable presence on social media to raise global awareness. Global diffusion of grievances and new forms of global solidarity animated renewed demands for political change.

Conclusions

The COVID-19 pandemic has provided a new set of challenges to contentious politics and social movements demanding political change and social justice. The pandemic both deepened and made more visible patterns of marginalization and also implicated governments for sustaining these forms of oppression. At the same time, the pandemic and consequent quarantine that brought many street protests around the world to a halt ignited a series of new demands and new forms of mobilization.

Contentious politics and social mobilization were at the center of the search for political transformation during the street protests of 2019 as well as in the innovative new forms of mobilization from cars, balconies, and on social media that characterized contentious politics in 2020. The pattern of mobilization followed by state repression followed by new repertoires of protest is visible around the world. While specific contexts and demands for justice vary widely, globalization and the diffusion of models is a core characteristic of these mobilizations. There are reasons to anticipate that post-pandemic contentious politics may empower those seeking transformation more than those conservatives seeking to shore up the status quo. As was true following early pandemics such as the Black Death, the violent and tragic disruption may usher in a new era of change and with it the potential for increased social justice. Social mobilization and contentious politics, a major force in driving transformation in 2019 and 2020, are likely to remain at the center of this transformation.

Given the many reasons to anticipate a lengthy and uneven period of recovery from the COVID-19 pandemic, it is difficult to predict with any certainty the how contentious encounters between people and states will evolve. The imperatives of protest movements to demonstrate power through size, unity, and steadfastness are likely to shape future forms of contention, with an increased focus on how these can be signaled through social media and other forms of new media. It is notable that despite tremendous pressures, most social movements in most of the world have remained overwhelmingly nonviolent. Riots and looting have certainly occurred, but given the scale and expanse of the protests, such disorder has been markedly limited. One-sided state violence remains extremely high in places ranging from the Philippines to Iraq and police brutality has been the focal point of mass movements in the United States and Brazil. However, there is little to suggest to date that those engaged in mass street protests are moving toward armed insurrection in most of the world. While demands for justice remain expansive, the favored tools – even in a time of pandemic – have been nonviolent mass mobilization.

Notes

1 Doug McAdam, Sidney Tarrow, and Charles Tilly, *The Dynamics of Contention* (Cambridge: Cambridge University Press, 2001).
2 Terrence Lyons and Peter Mandaville, *Politics from Afar: Transnational Diasporas and Networks* (New York: Oxford University Press, 2012).
3 "Contextualizing the Arab Awakenings: An Exclusive Interview with Srjda Popovic," *Journal of Middle Eastern Politics and Policy*, April 14, 2014, https://jmepp.hkspublications.org/2014/04/18/contextualizing-the-arab-awakenings-an-exclusive-interview-with-srjda-popovic/.
4 Agnieszka Paczynska, "Cross-Regional Comparisons: The Arab Uprisings as Political Transitions and Social Movements," *Perspectives on Politics* 46, no. 2 (April 2013): 217–21.
5 Gaby Hinaliff, "'The Rapist Is You!': Why a Chilean Protest Chant Is Being Sung Around the World," *The Guardian*, February 3, 2020, www.theguardian.com/society/2020/feb/03/the-rapist-is-you-chilean-protest-song-chanted-around-the-world-un-iolador-en-tu-camino; Harmeet Kaur, "In Protests Around the World, One Image Stands Out: The Joker," *CNN*, November 3, 2019, www.cnn.com/2019/11/03/world/joker-global-protests-trnd/index.html.
6 Vivian Wang, Maria Abi-Habib, and Vivian Yee, "'This Government Is Lucky': Coronavirus Quiets Global Protest Movements," *New York Times*, April 23, 2020, www.nytimes.com/2020/04/23/world/asia/coronavirus-protest-hong-kong-india-lebanon.html.

7 Laura Spinney, *Pale Rider: The Spanish Flue of 1918 and How It Changed the World* (New York: Public Affairs, 2017).
8 We thank Fatma Jabbari for her assistance in developing this section.
9 Saskia Brechenmacher, Thomas Carothers, and Richard Youngs, "Civil Society and the Coronavirus: Dynamism Despite Disruption," *Carnegie Endowment for International Peace*, April 21, 2020, https://carnegieendowment.org/2020/04/21/civil-society-and-coronavirus-dynamism-despite-disruption-pub-81592.
10 Claudia Ciobanu, "Poles Find Creative Ways to Protest Despite the Pandemic," April 21, 2020, https://balkaninsight.com/2020/04/21/poles-find-creative-ways-to-protest-despite-the-pandemic/.
11 Charles McGowan, "How Quarantined Chileans Are Keeping Their Protest Movement Alive," *Al Jazeera*, April 14, 2020, www.aljazeera.com/indepth/features/quarantined-chileans-keeping-protest-movement-alive-200414122141809.html.
12 See Reuters, "Lebanese Protesters Return to Streets in Car Convoys Amid Coronavirus Lockdown," April 21, 2020, www.reuters.com/article/us-health-coronavirus-lebanon-protests/lebanese-protesters-return-to-streets-in-car-convoys-amid-coronavirus-lockdown-idUSKCN2232WK.
13 Vitali Shkliarov, "Belurus Is Having an Anti-'Cockroach' Revolution," *Foreign Policy*, June 4, 2020, https://foreignpolicy.com/2020/06/04/belarus-protest-vote-lukashenko-stop-cockroach/.

5 Migration and the COVID-19 pandemic

Omar Grech

The current crisis has already caused significant shifts in the global flow of migrants from South to North – shifts that will be challenged as economic recovery increases enterprise demand for migrant labor, while local populations may resist restarting immigration even more strongly than in pre-COVID days. The author, an expert on human rights and migration in the Euro-Mediterranean region, describes that impact of this potentially fierce conflict on Northern economies and on the human rights of migrants. The essay concludes by offering insights as to how can the conflict be resolved without serious civil violence.

Introduction

Migratory flows across the world have been an issue of debate and controversy well before the outbreak of the COVID-19 pandemic.[1] International attention to the challenges posed by managing migration both sensibly and humanely have been the cause of tension within communities and also between states.[2] In this context, many countries across the world have taken increasingly restrictive measures in terms of not allowing unauthorized migrants to enter their jurisdictions. Furthermore, social tensions and even episodes of physical violence within communities hosting higher concentrations of migrants have been evident in numerous destination countries.

The outbreak of the pandemic has already impacted the management of migration and also attitudes toward it in multiple ways. The two most evident, immediate impacts of COVID-19 relate to (i) the effects of the public health measures on the national and global economies and (ii) free movement within and across states. This chapter suggests that the economic repercussions of the pandemic may have serious consequences on migratory flows and the management of migration. Moreover, the suspension of various fundamental human rights and freedoms during the crisis may have longer-term consequences on the attitudes toward migrants in host countries.

It is also worth noting that, from a medical perspective, the pandemic has impacted most heavily on marginalized and impoverished communities, of which migrants (especially recent migrants) inevitably form a part. The fatalities among migrant groups are among the highest in most destination countries. Lack of access to health services as well as other social services and poorer living conditions, have, *inter alia*, caused migrants to suffer disproportionately from COVID-19.[3] These conditions are risk factors which may well be aggravated further for migrant communities in the coming years.

This chapter, in summary, seeks to explore likely pandemic-generated scenarios with respect to migratory flows[4] and the integration of migrants in host countries, including their human rights. In conclusion, it seeks to suggest ways in which the potential for conflict in the context of migration may be attenuated.

The impact of COVID-19 on countries of origin

All economic forecasts by international agencies anticipate that the aftermath of the pandemic will see an increase of economic deprivation with global recession impacting directly for at least the next 2/3 years, but with longer-term effects considered likely. The effects of the recession will impact countries of origin both directly and indirectly: directly through the internal economic slowdown which may also see lower levels of Overseas Development Assistance from developed countries, which will very well tighten their development assistance budgets; indirectly, countries of origin may lose a very valuable input in their economies through the probable loss of a portion of the income received from remittances of migrant workers. Migrant labor in the EU and USA for instance will probably be among the most severely affected communities in terms of the economic crisis. The likelihood of a reduction in remittances from migrant workers has already been highlighted by international agencies.[5] The levels of Foreign Direct Investment in the countries of origin may also decrease, at least in the short term. All of these factors are, in turn, likely to increase the number of economic migrants toward areas such as the USA, EU, and Australia.

The other key driver of migration apart from economic factors is violent conflict. The extent to which forced migration resulting from conflict (i.e. refugees) will be impacted by COVID-19 is more difficult to assess. Early indications show that the pandemic caused a decrease in the number of conflict-related violence during the pandemic.[6] The extent and duration of this conflict "slowdown" is too early to forecast. In this context, it would be useful for conflict resolution specialists to examine the conflict data in order to verify the extent of the slowdown in violence and also the exact drivers of this slowdown. If the decrease in violence is sustained, this may also lead to some decrease in the levels of conflict-related refugee flows. Conversely, if the levels of violent conflict return to pre-pandemic levels or even increase further, the flow of refugees will also necessarily increase. It is important to recall that these increased flows impact first and foremost the surrounding countries in the immediate vicinity of the conflict zones.[7]

This latter point merits emphasis as the migratory flows should not just be seen in the context of destination countries in the more economically developed areas such as Europe and North America. In examining post-pandemic migratory flows, one must consider the fact that migration from countries of origin will quite likely increase in both volume and impact on other developing countries. In this context, the post-pandemic approach to the environment and climate change will also be of crucial importance in attenuating or exacerbating the issue of climate change refugees.

The impact of COVID-19 on destination countries

The pandemic has impacted the countries of destination in a number of ways with the economic downturn being the most obvious one. This is evident in two of the main areas of incoming migration: Europe and North America. The effects of the recession will likely have a long duration, not only just statistically but also at the level of perception.

The recession has already caused significant unemployment globally and the magnitude of this is likely to increase. The International Labour Organization is anticipating a loss of over 300 million jobs worldwide with Europe and the Americas being among the worst hit.[8] In this context, young people are expected to suffer most severely from these job losses and those in operating in the informal economy are set to be significantly hit. With migrants being predominantly young[9] and operating most intensely in the informal sectors, the likelihood of migrants being particularly hit by COVID-19-related unemployment is acute.

This increase in unemployment rates is also set to have a severe impact on the public coffers with more requests for unemployment benefit and other social support. During the early stages of the pandemic, some countries witnessed a decrease of foreign workers with some returning to their countries of origin. These movements, however, are more related to returns to middle-income countries.

The economic downturn will naturally have repercussions on both migrants and locals. For migrants whose status is not regularized and who have no access to social services, the impact may be devastating. Migrant communities have already suffered more heavily from the health aspects of the pandemic and from the measures taken by host countries to deal with the pandemic.[10] If this is coupled with an over-impact of the economic crisis, the levels of frustration and desperation may well lead to some forms of violence.

For local communities, increases in levels of unemployment and decreases in levels of disposable income may likewise cause social discontent. The tendency to perceive migrants as being too numerous and that they cannot be integrated socially and economically may also increase in a post-COVID world of economic decline and booming unemployment.[11]

In an environment where feelings of insecurity are growing, the "migrants steal our jobs" mentality may only be exacerbated irrespective of its factual basis. In Europe and the USA, leaders from the so-called populist right had already resorted to stoking these feelings prior to the pandemic. The anti-immigration rhetoric adopted by the Trump Campaign in 2016 with the promise to build "The Wall" (reiterated during his administration),[12] or the language of "Prima gli italiani" (Italians First) adopted by the League in Italy[13] or the promise to fight the "invasion of foreigners" expressed by Alternative für Deutschland,[14] in Germany, are likely to be exploited even more markedly in the coming years. With the economic downturn and its attendant hardships, the number of people attracted by this rhetoric could increase exponentially. Within such a context, the potential of social tensions spilling into violence, including violence against migrants, becomes more acute.[15]

COVID-19 has also modified attitudes toward borders and human movement in general. The closure of airports and ports, coupled with the drastic reduction in opportunities for travel, may impact the perceptions of some toward human movement. In particular, the idea that dangers come from outside national frontiers (which was already discernible in some sectors of the local populations) may have extended to many more as a result of the restrictive measures taken in the context of the pandemic. Even more directly, several governments used the COVID-19-related emergency powers to block the entry of migrants, including asylum seekers, into their territories[16] in breach of international legal rules. The risks of such powers and practices being retained are real, especially if a vaccine is not developed. This would allow states to continue citing the virus as an excuse for such practices on public health grounds.

In this context, a broad reflection on how the pandemic has impacted our attitudes toward fundamental human rights is warranted. The public health emergency led to the suspension of various fundamental human rights such as freedom of association and freedom of movement. What impact have these suspensions had on our commitment to human rights both individually and collectively? Has the pandemic left a legacy of disregard for the fundamental rights of migrants in the name of public health considerations or more general national exigencies? Moreover, will these public health-related suspensions tempt governments to abuse more frequently fundamental rights, especially with reference to migrants and asylum seekers? These are risks which need to be considered and addressed. In this respect, human rights NGOs and international human rights agencies should monitor closely the extent to which states are abiding by their national laws and their international obligations in this regard.

Implications for action

In the scenarios described earlier, what are the possible actions that can reduce the possibility of social tension and violence? From a structural perspective, the pandemic will provide an opportunity to reassess the way we manage our economies nationally and globally. In the post-pandemic phase, principles of social justice and fairness are more relevant than ever. The pandemic has clearly hit some sections of our communities much more severely than others both health-wise and economically. If in the post-pandemic phase these inequalities are not addressed or are even exacerbated, the risks of a "war between the poor" in the form of conflict between the worst-hit locals and the migrant communities, will become more likely. Post-pandemic the current dominant model of economic growth at all costs will only increase tension and possible conflict if expected inequalities arise.

A sense of public commitment to practical solidarity toward those who have suffered most during the pandemic should help in addressing the sentiments of frustration and despair felt by those communities who have seen their lives and their livelihoods most imperiled. One of the key divides in most destination countries is that between locals who have benefited from globalization (in all its facets) and those who have not. The success of populist politics hinges on this divide to a substantial extent. This divide has been expressed in various ways in the different countries, but always broadly categorizing the local people who educationally, socially, and economically have done well as against those who have not. Those who have not, feel aggrieved that their concerns and interests have been side-lined.

This sense of grievance will be exacerbated if they perceive that the pandemic has left them further behind. In a post-pandemic world, those who feel ignored or left behind must be put center stage of the socio-economic recovery. For instance, fears held by sections of these communities around the negative impact of migrants on their employment prospects should be addressed. The impact of migrants on the employment and wage prospects of native-born workers will be different in different regions. However, there is some evidence that while migrant workers generally do not impact employment prospects, this may happen in certain regions during periods of economic recession and that migrant workers may push down wages for the less skilled workforce.[17] Wherever such possibilities arise governments must resort to remedial policies in cooperation with local trade unions. Such measures could include adequately monitored minimum wage requirements that avoid wage undercutting. Where there are no such impacts, governments, and civil society need to be proactive in demonstrating this.

The populist narrative of "our citizens first" can be countered with a counternarrative focusing on shared humanity and attendant human solidarity. The chances of success of such a counternarrative, however, will be higher in societies where a sense of fairness and justice is flourishing. Societies, which are broadly seen to safeguard the interests of the unfortunate as well as the fortunate, will have a better opportunity to promote narratives of solidarity with those who are coming from across borders. Efforts to contend with the anti-migrant narratives should also engage with anti-hate speech movement, which has acquired greater salience in recent years. This momentum needs to be maintained and even invigorated using political campaigns, legal instruments, and heightened citizen engagement.

In all of these efforts, conflict resolution practitioners have a role to play. This role is multifaceted. The interaction between human rights and conflict resolution, the relationship between social justice and peacebuilding as well as the use of conflict resolution techniques in bringing together migrant communities and host communities are all areas of expertise that can be utilized constructively in this context.

Finally, it is important to acknowledge the positive contribution that a return to "normality" may have in some of these migration-related challenges. In this context, the development of a vaccine would play a fundamental role in a return to daily lives. The discovery of a vaccine would probably encourage a swifter economic recovery, with related benefits to employment rates and livelihoods. A return to normality would also see a return to a daily life where travel is again a normal and desirable reality, where governments have no public health grounds to limit anyone's human rights and where human interaction returns to pre-pandemic models. In such an eventuality, the novel concept of social distancing should give way to the ancient concept of human embrace. This can only have a positive impact on how we look at each other and particularly at those who come from afar.

Notes

1 The challenges posed by migratory flows both internationally and nationally led the UN to promote the adoption of the Global Compact on Migration.

See the Resolution adopted by the United Nations General Assembly on 19 December 2018.

2 See for example the USA-Mexico diatribe around migrants passing through the Mexico-USA border or the tensions between Spain, France, Italy and Malta about the responsibility for saving and then taking responsibility for migrants crossing the Mediterranean on vessels.

3 For example, see accessed June 23, 2020, www.theguardian.com/world/2020/may/18/coronavirus-crisis-increases-suffering-of-most-vulnerable-refugees.

4 In terms of both countries of origin and destination countries.

5 The World Bank, "World Bank Predicts Sharpest Decline of Remittances in Recent History," April 22, 2020, accessed June 14, 2020, www.world bank.org/en/news/press-release/2020/04/22/world-bank-predicts-sharpest-decline-of-remittances-in-recent-history.

6 This decrease is reported in the ACLED database, accessed June 17, 2020, https://acleddata.com/#/dashboard.

7 For example, the UNHCR estimates that the conflict in South Sudan has created "over two million South Sudanese refugees, mainly in Ethiopia, Sudan, and Uganda". See accessed June 17, 2020, www.unhcr.org/south-sudan-emergency.html#:~:text=Inside%20South%20Sudan%2C%20nearly%20two,or%20struggle%20with%20food%20insecurity.

8 International Labour Organization, "ILO Monitor: COVID-19 and the World of Work," April 29, 2020, accessed June 17, 2020, www.ilo.org/wcmsp5/groups/public/-dgreports/-dcomm/documents/briefingnote/wcms_743146.pdf.

9 For example, half of the immigrants moving into the EU in 2018 were under 29 years of age, accessed June 9, 2020, https://ec.europa.eu/eurostat/statistics-explained/index.php/Migration_and_migrant_population_statistics.

10 For example, in Greece riots erupted in May 2020 at a migrant processing centre due to delays in processing asylum claims, accessed June 14, 2020, www.dailysabah.com/politics/violent-protest-erupts-at-greece-migrant-center-near-turkey-border/news.

11 The sentiment that immigration should not increase was already wiely felt before the pandemic emerged. A 2018 Pew Research survey showed more opposed increased migration than thought the same levels of migration should be maintained or increased. See accessed June 14, 2020, www.pewresearch.org/fact-tank/2018/12/10/many-worldwide-oppose-more-migration-both-into-and-out-of-their-countries/.

12 The Guardian, Donald Trump's border wall speech – in full, January 9, 2019, accessed June 14, 2020, www.theguardian.com/us-news/2019/jan/09/donald-trumps-border-wall-speech-in-full.

13 Il Messaggero, "Migranti, Salvini, Prima gli italiani, chi la pensa in maniera diversa voti M5S," April 25, 2019, accessed June 14, 2020, www.ilmessaggero.it/politica/di_maio_salvini_migranti-4451555.html.

14 BBC, "Germany's AfD: How Right-Wing Is Nationalist Alternative for Germany?," January 20, 2020, accessed June 14, 2020, www.bbc.com/news/world-europe-37274201.

15 Pre-COVID protests against immigration have already witnessed episodes of violence, see BBC, "Brussels Protest Over UN Migration Pact Turns Violent," December 16, 2018, accessed June 14, 2020, www.bbc.com/news/world-europe-46585237.

16 For example Malta and Italy within the EU declared their ports unsafe in the context of the pandemic and refused entry to migrants even when the latter were claiming to be asylum seekers. See EU Observer, "EU Unable to Comment on Italy and Malta Port Closures," April 15, 2020, accessed June 14, 2020, https://euobserver.com/migration/148058.

17 BBC, "Reality Check: Do Foreign Workers Take Jobs and Cut Wages?," October 6, 2016, accessed June 20, 2020, www.bbc.com/news/business-37577620.

6 COVID-19 and nationalism

Karina V. Korostelina

The decade leading up to the current biomedical and economic crises was marked by a strong resurgence in global nationalist sentiment: a highly decentralized multinational movement sometimes referred to as right-wing populism. In some ways, the crisis has served to reinforce the trend toward nationalist identity, while in others its effects may well be to undermine "go it alone" nationalism by strengthening broader regional, civilizational, and even human identities. This chapter analyzes the factors that are most likely to determine one set of outcomes or the other and describes roles that can conflict resolvers may play in fostering more inclusive senses of political identity.

Introduction

The rise of nationalism during the current COVID-19 pandemic was noted by many academics, journalists, and political commentators. Most of them also discuss the increase in discriminatory policies and exclusion of various groups based on their citizenship status or ethnic/religious origin. Based on the analysis of the dynamics of nationalism on the global, national, and identity group levels, this paper posits that COVID-19 will create deeper disagreements and provoke tensions between globalists and nationalists on the global and national levels. With the pandemic exacerbating the criticism of international organizations and anti-EU sentiments, the societies become more divided in their vision of international cooperation. While a majority of people support the temporary closure of borders within their countries, the processes of reopening could provoke more tensions and exclusions. New restrictions on civil liberties and rising unemployment can empower right-wing and mainstream conservative parties in democratic societies and promote the expansion of surveillance in authoritarian ones. Discriminatory and exclusionary policies toward minorities and immigrants could become the most important long-term effect of the current crisis.

Nationalism and pandemics

The academic literature on the relations between pandemics and nationalisms is surprisingly scarce, given that several recent waves of such viral infections as SARS (severe acute respiratory syndrome), MERS (Middle East respiratory syndrome), and Ebola and Zika viruses (Madhav et al., 2018)[1] have occurred. Some studies emphasize the effects of nationalism on health policies during pandemics in a single country. As Sung-Won describes in his analysis of the SARS pandemic in China, nationalism had a significant impact on political decision-making as well as on the design and implementation of health policies, justifying tough regulatory measures and securitization of the public health by the need to restore national pride and to secure China's national interests. At the same time, in order to unite the entire nation and increase loyalty to the state, the propaganda department posited the SARS pandemic as a national crisis. Balasegaram and Schnur (2006)[2] also discuss the rising national mobilization and rhetoric of nationalism in China during the SARS pandemic. Similarly, the 1918–1919 influenza pandemic- the deadliest in Iran's twentieth-century history – had provoked the rise of Iranian nationalism and a break with the western institutions responsible for public health*.

Several studies have explored the links between nation-building, nationalism, and pandemics. Some stress the interrelations between the efforts to control disease and the rise of the modern state and nationalism (Harrison, 2004),[3] while others focus on the social and cultural construction of disease as a tool justifying the power of a state (Hays, 2009),[4] the impact of pandemics on national institutions (Spinney, 2017)[5] and the growing divisions between globalists and nationalists with the rise of pandemics (Van Toorn, 2020).[6] In his overview of global nationalism in the time of COVID, Bieber (2020)[7] discusses the recent trajectory of nationalism, analyzing the interrelationship between nationalism, growing authoritarianism, and deglobalization, as well as increase in biases and fear. Similarly, Fukuyama (2020)[8] opines that the COVID-19 pandemic will contribute to the growing nationalism, isolationism, xenophobia, and attacks on the liberal world.

In this case, as in others, the analysis of ongoing social processes is complicated by incomplete data, constantly changing environments, and a prevalence of politically charged interpretations. The systemic approach is a useful tool for researching complex, multilevel phenomena such as nationalism, because it helps to find knowledge gaps in a situation of rapidly changing social reality and to define areas of ambiguity for better understanding of future impacts. The study of nationalism as a system requires analysis on several levels: (1) the transformation of nationalism within the wider system of international relations, globalization, and anti-globalization processes; (2) current dynamics of the doctrine within national borders; and (3) the transformation of such subsystems as immigration policies, discrimination against minorities, and other patterns of exclusion.

Anti-globalism and COVID-19

The anti-globalism of the last decade differs from the "economic justice" anti-globalization movement of the 1990s and 2000s, as it is: (1) right-wing and conservative in its nature, (2) a mix of cultural and economic discontents, emphasizing dangers of cultural and racial mixing, and (3) channeling the disappointment with "cosmopolitan" elites through presentation of immigrants and other undeserving groups as a threat (Voelz, 2017).[9] It is a response to the neoliberal approach to globalization that was promoted by center-left parties across North America and Europe and that eventually cost them a good share of votes. The new reality of the global pandemic increases the primacy of the state, challenging neoliberal policies and positioning global cooperation and international movement of population as causal factors that allow the rapid spread of COVID-19 across national boundaries. As the states have secured medical supplies for their citizens and raised barriers to international trade, the role of the free market as a regulator of economic needs has decreased in salience.

A majority of studies present anti-globalism as a form of political *populism* that unites the horizontal cultural dimension of xenophobia with its vertical anti-elitist dimensions. This sort of conservative populism positions elites as biased in favor of outgroups, promotes nativism and an exclusive national identity, and elevates the role of the state in ensuring the security of its citizens through protectionist economic policies and opposition to immigration (Alberta, 2017; Brubaker, 2017; Hoover, 2019; Mudde 2017; Oliver and Rahn, 2016).[10] Other authors assert that the phenomenon represents a transition within *fascism* from a supremacist to a separatist ideology (Bessner and Sparke 2017; Giroux, 2018; Judis, 2016).[11] A growing number of scholars analyzes anti-globalism as a form of *paleoconservatism* that describes how the managerial state undermined and homogenized traditional and bourgeois worldviews in the institutions of Western society. Paleoconservatism promotes restrictions on immigration, reduces foreign commitments and democracy promotion, and scales back foreign aid (Beiner, 2018; Drolet and Williams 2019; O'Meara 2013).[12]

The COVID-19 pandemic intensified these voices of anti-globalism, giving them an opportunity to use the rapid spread of a disease as a reason to restrict cross-border initiatives and programs, criticize transnational governance structures, and restate nationalism by introducing national "health strategies." Over 70 countries employed "medical nationalism" (Youde, 2020)[13] that prioritizes national needs, securitizes public health, puts restrictions on the export of medical supplies and medications, and downplays international cooperation. The effects of such policies are manifold. The slow response of the EU countries and the imposed limits on the export of protective medical equipment to Italy strongly contributed to the Euro-criticism that was already boosted by Brexit (Boffey, 2020).[14] As a result, polls found that 42% of Italians wanted to exit the European Union and that 59% saw the EU as meaningless (Amaro, 2020).[15] However, in Germany, by contrast, 59% saw globalization as advantageous to their country (Poushter and Schumacher, 2020).[16]

The internal divide within the EU, resulting from international policies related to the pandemic, is echoed by the political divide within the United States. According to the April 2020 polls (Poushter and Schumacher, 2020), Americans are about evenly divided in positive or negative view of globalization (47% vs. 44%). Similarly, Americans are split in their view of post-outbreak international cooperation: with 34% expecting no change in the extent to which countries cooperate with one another, 35% expecting countries to increase their focus on cooperation, and 29% expecting more focus on countries' own national interest (Mordecai 2020).[17] Americans also are divided in their assessment of the World Health Organization, with 62% of Democrats and Democratic-leaning independents positively assessing its job in handling the pandemic and 70% of Republicans and GOP leaner's viewing it negatively (Moncus and Connaughton, 2020).[18] The withdrawal of the United States from the WHO and the rising role of China in international organizations can change the meaning and the functioning of international cooperation, moving away from the core of North Atlantic collaboration. Thus, in Germany, people increasingly want their country to cooperate with China rather than the United States (36% and 37%, respectively, in 2020 compared with 50% vs. 24% in 2019) (Poushter and Schumacher, 2020).

Nationalism within national borders

Nationalism and particularism are seen by right-wing parties as cures for the social troubles related to globalization. Nationalism is one of the major mechanisms of national identity formation through the processes of state-building (Gelner 1983; Hobsbawm, 1990)[19] and supports the manipulations of national ideas by political and social elites to obtain and legitimize state power (Brubaker, 2017).[20] Nationalism is rooted in such mechanisms of the formation of national identity as the communal imagination and politicization of history (Anderson, 1991; Smith, 2011).[21] Both processes of nationalism – the construction and the employment of national identity – are used by far-right parties to promote exclusionary nationalism (Bieber 2020a) and ethnic concept of national identity (Korostelina, 2007).[22]

The COVID-19 pandemic has provided these parties a fresh opportunity to go beyond the usual populist themes of fighting corruption and an alien elite, threats of immigration and Islam, and loss of jobs to foreign countries. However, as Mudde (2020) analyzes, the response of populist and far-right leaders to COVID-19 differs significantly across countries: the United States, Brazil, and Mexico tend to underplay the seriousness of the medical crisis and to provide slow responses; the Netherlands and India have advocated for immediate lockdown policies, and Hungary and Israel are establishing emergency policies that sideline established political institutions. Nevertheless, despite the differences in the timing or a form of the response, these elites use the claim of citizens protection from the pandemics to prioritize national interests. At least 91% of the world's population lives in countries with restrictions on people arriving from other countries who are neither citizens nor residents, and 39% live in countries with completely closed borders (Connor, 2020).[23]

Many scholars and political commentators recently expressed the concern that the closure of the borders and suppression of civil liberties will continue well beyond the COVID-19 pandemics and contribute to protectionism, isolationism, and exclusive nationalism (e.g., Allen, et al. 2020; Fukuyama 2020).[24] Some tendencies in public opinion show the preference of national interests and the agreement with the restrictions. For example, 95% of Americans supported restricting international travel to the United States (Pew Research Center 2020a).[25] The survey conducted in the UK in April 2020 shows the clear preference of the public to address the COVID-19 within the country (80% of respondents) rather than providing help to developing countries (17%) and poor countries (15%) (YouGov 2020).[26]

However, as Bieber (2020) aptly stated, while the continuous global spread of the pandemic can sustain border restrictions aimed at travelers from the Global South, it is unlikely that both the governments and national populations will support such measures in the long term. The main concern is that the narrative of restoring civil liberties and lifting the lockdown will be hijacked by the right-wing and mainstream conservative parties, while progressive political forces fail to promptly respond to this tendency, losing control over the democratic processes (Youngs, 2020).[27] The recent polls show that concerns over COVID-19 in 27 countries are declining (from 63% in April to 47% in June), while concerns over unemployment are on the rise (from 35% in April to 42% in June), with the highest level of concerns demonstrated in Italy (66%), Spain (65%) and South Korea (63%) (Gebrekal, 2020).[28] The process of the border opening also can exacerbate ethnic and international tensions. For example, the exclusion of Serbia from the list of open borders with Montenegro based on the number of COVID-19 cases sparked an angry response in Serbia (AP 2020).[29]

Immigration and minorities

The policies of the emergency response to the pandemic have targeted several groups of populations, including minorities, migrants within a country, and potential immigrants and asylum seekers. The fear of deadly virus together with economic crisis and lockdown-related depression and anxiety contributed to the vicious cycle of "frustration-aggression," scapegoating, and dehumanization. First, together with the linking of the virus to China by politicians and public officials in multiple countries including the United States, Italy, and Brazil, the frustration of the lockdown and increased unemployment resulted in verbal and physical assaults, and discrimination against individuals of Chinese origin or Asians in general (Human Rights Watch, 2020).[30] The COVID-19 pandemic also increased discrimination and attacks on groups that were blamed for the disease and labeled as "spreaders" or "supercarriers," for example, Muslims in India, Sri Lanka, Myanmar, and Middle East, and Roma in Central Europe (Human Rights Watch, 2020).

Second, the public health emergency situation has justified drastic measures against some migrants within the country. For example, in the United States, the Department of Homeland Security returned illegal and undocumented migrants to their countries of origin without due process based on "the authority to rapidly return individuals that could potentially be infected with COVID-19" (CBP, 2020).[31] U.S. public opinion also reflected the exclusion of and establishment of rigid social boundaries vis-a-vis immigrants: while 68% of U.S. adults supported federal medical care for undocumented immigrants ill with the coronavirus, only 37% approved economic aid to undocumented immigrants who had lost their job due to the outbreak (Krogstad and Lopez, 2020).

Third, some nations have banned entry by asylum seekers, including Hungary, where Viktor Orbán linked COVID-19 to immigrants, the United States, which turned away potential asylum seekers at its southern border, Canada, which stopped hearings for asylum seekers entering by land from the United States, and Greece, which suspended new applications for asylum (Connor, 2020). Claiming to protect 525,000 jobs for Americans, "prioritizing getting them back into the labor supply and getting them to work and standing on their own two feet again," President Trump announced the executive order of suspension of immigration and new temporary work visas till the end of 2020 amid the coronavirus pandemic (Hackman, 2020).[32] In Denmark, the inability to execute the naturalization law that requires a handshake with the official granting citizenship, has resulted in a temporal deferral of naturalization (Bieber, 2020).

Concluding remarks

The emergency responses to the COVID-19 pandemic have brought sweeping changes across the globe, deepening disagreements, and provoking conflicts between globalists and nationalists. Together with the increasing criticism of international organizations, societies become more divided in their visions of the future of international cooperation, sharpening the tensions between globalists and nationalists. The anti-EU sentiments in some countries may also grow, unless Germany takes advantage of its new EU Presidency and contributes to the development of a strengthened and more dynamic EU.

While the closing of national borders has a short-term effect, the processes of reopening can promote more exclusions and exacerbate already existing conflicts between ethnic and national groups. In democratic societies, the public frustration related to limited civil liberties, lockdowns, and rising unemployment can give a boost to the right-wing and mainstream conservative parties if progressive political forces do not produce an effective response. In more authoritarian societies, the expansion of surveillance can continue well beyond the pandemics.

The process of blaming migrants or minorities for disease is well-described in academic literature and is linked to increasing discriminatory and exclusionary policies. Thus, the cumulative bias against minorities and immigrants as well as their marginalization and inequality could remain well beyond the pandemic's recession. The limitation on immigration and temporary work visas can remain for a long time, adding to the populist rhetoric of protecting jobs from immigrants.

Can these tendencies be reversed? Quite possibly, but to reverse them will require new thinking and strategic action on the part of globalists. Instead of assuming, with theorists such as Habermas and Fukayama, that the triumph of liberalism is inevitable, the advocates of global solutions should engage in deep debates with the proponents of right-wing ideology, understanding that the current popularity of their views reflects unsatisfied needs for economic security and communal solidarity as well as a retrograde tribalism. How can cosmopolitan progressives offer to satisfy these legitimate needs? Clearly, not simply by pledging allegiance to existing global elites or abstract universalist ideals. Globalism needs to be reconceptualized in ways that demonstrate the efficacy of transnational ideas and institutions to solve local problems ranging from the precarious existence of many workers, farmers, and entrepreneurs to the cultural insecurities produced by rapid modernization.

Many people turned to right-wing nationalists because nobody else seemed to be listening to their complaints. Fortunately, a rethinking of globalist assumptions and methods of discourse with this problem in mind has already begun (see, for example, Joseph E. Stiglitz, 2017).[33] Theorists now understand that globalization is not simply a euphemism for free trade. Mass support for transnational concepts and practices regarding human rights, social equality, religious freedom, and economic development exists, so long as it is understood that the relationship of global trends to local norms is a matter requiring negotiation rather than being decided by fiat. Local communities must have a meaningful voice in such negotiations, and conflict resolution specialists have a vital role to play in making sure that all stakeholder voices are heard. Through such efforts, it may then become clear that globalization and local empowerment are not diametrical opposites but potential partners in the betterment of communal life.

Notes

1 N. Madhav, B. Oppenheim, M. Galivan, P. Mulembakani, E. Rubin, and N. Wolfe, "Pandemics: Risks, Impacts, and Mitigation," in *Disease Control Priorities: Improving Health and Reducing Poverty*, ed. D. T. Jamison, R. Nugent, H. Gelband, S. Horton, P. Jha, R. Laxminarayan, C. N. Mock, 3rd ed., Vol. 9 (Washington, DC: World Bank, 2018).

2 M. Balasegaram and A. Schnur, "China: From Denial to Mass Mobilization," in *SARS: How A Global Epidemic Was Stopped* (Geneva: WHO, 2006), 73–85.

3 M. Harrison, *Disease and the Modern World: 1500 to the Present Day* (Cambridge: Polity, 2004).

4 J. N. Hays, *The Burden of Disease: Epidemics and Human Response in Western History*, rev. ed. (New Brunswick, NJ: Rutgers University Press, 2009).

5 L. Spinney, *Pale Rider: The Spanish Flu of 1918 and How It Changed the World* (New York: Public Affairs, 2010).

6 T. Van Toorn, "Life After the Pandemic: Future Scenarios," *Diplomatic Courier* (2020): 148–52.

7 F. Bieber, "Global Nationalism in Times of the COVID-19 Pandemic," *Nationalities Papers* (2020): 1–13, doi:10.1017/nps.2020.35; F. Bieber, *Debating Nationalism: The Global Spread of Nations* (London: Bloomsbury Press, 2020); M. O'Meara, *New Culture, New Right: Anti-Liberalism in Postmodern Europe* (London: Artkos, 2013).

8 F. Fukuyama, "The Pandemic and Political Order: It Takes a State," *Foreign Affairs*, Council for Foreign Affairs, 2020. https://www.foreignaffairs.com/articles/world/2020-06-09/pandemic-and-political-order.

9 J. Voelz, "Transnationalism and Anti-Globalism," *College Literature* 44, no. 4 (2017).

10 Tim Alberta, "Donald Trump and the Evangelical-Nationalist Alliance," *Politico*, October 14, 2017, accessed June 9, 2020, www.politico.com/magazine/story/2017/10/14/trump-evangelical-nationalist-alliance-215713; D. R. Hoover, "Populism and Internationalism, Evangelical Style," *The Review of Faith and International Affairs* 17, no. 3 (2019); C. Mudde, "Will the Coronavirus 'Kill Populism'? Don't Count on It," *The Guardian*, 2020, accessed June 11, 2020, www.theguardian.com/commentisfree/2020/mar/27/coronavirus-populism-trump-politics-response; J. E. Oliver and W. M. Rahn, "Rise of the *Trumpenvolk:* Populism in the 2016 Election," *Annals of the American Academy of Political and Social Science* 667, no. 1 (2016): 189–206, doi:10.1177/0002716216662639.

11 D. Bessner and M. Sparke, "Nazism, Neoliberalism, and the Trumpist Challenge to Democracy," *Environment and Planning A: Economy and Space* 49, no. 6 (2017): 1214–23, doi:10.1177/0308518X17701429; H. Giroux, *The Public in Peril: Trump and the Menace of American Authoritarianism* (New York: Routledge, 2018); J. Judis, *The Populist Explosion: How the Great Recession Transformed American and European Politics* (New York: Columbia Global Reports, 2016).

12 R. Beiner, *Dangerous Minds: Nietzsche, Heidegger, and the Return of the Far Right* (Philadelphia: University of Pennsylvania Press, 2018); J. F. Drolet and M. Williams, "The View from MARS: US Paleoconservatism and Ideological Challenges to the Liberal World Order," *Canada's Journal of Global Policy Analysis* 74, no. 1 (2019).

13 J. Youde, "How medical nationalism is undermining the fight against the coronavirus pandemic," https://www.worldpoliticsreview.com/articles/28623.

14 D. Boffey, "Italy Criticizes EU for Being Slow to Help Over Coronavirus Epidemic," *The Guardian*, 2020, accessed June 12, 2020, www.theguardian.com/world/2020/mar/11/italy-criticises-eu-being-slow-help-coronavirus-epidemic.

15 S. Amaro, "Coronavirus Deepens Political Fragmentation in Italy as Anti-EU Sentiment Rises," *CNBC*, 2020, accessed June 15, 2020, www.cnbc.com/2020/04/21/italys-political-fragmentation-rises-amid-coronavirus-pandemic.html.

16 J. Poushter and S. Schumacher, "Amid Coronavirus Crisis, Americans and Germans See Changing World in Different Ways," 2020, accessed June 12, 2020, www.pewresearch.org/staff/jacob-poushter/.

17 M. Mordecai, "How Americans Envision a Post-Pandemic World Order," *Pew Research Center*, 2020, accessed June 14, 2020, www.pewresearch.org/fact-tank/2020/06/02/how-americans-envision-a-post-pandemic-world-order/.

18 J. Moncus and A. Connaughton, "Americans' Views on World Health Organization Split Along Partisan Lines as Trump Calls for U.S. to Withdraw," *Pew Research Center*, 2020, accessed June 27, 2020, www.pewresearch.org/fact-tank/2020/06/11/americans-views-on-world-health-organization-split-along-partisan-lines-as-trump-calls-for-u-s-to-withdraw/.

19 E. Gellner, *Nations and Nationalism* (Ithaca: Cornell University Press, 1983); E. J. Hobsbawm, *Nations and Nationalism Since 1780: Programme, Myth, Reality* (Cambridge: Cambridge University Press, 1990).

20 R. Brubaker, "Between Nationalism and Civilizationism: The European Populist Moment in Comparative Perspective," *Ethnic and Racial Studies* 40, no. 8 (2017): 1191–226, doi:10.1080/01419870.2017.1294700

21 B. Anderson, *Imagined Communities: Reflections on the Origin and Spread of Nationalism* (London: Verso, 1991); A. D. Smith, "National Identity and Vernacular Mobilisation in Europe," *Nations and Nationalism* 17, no. 2 (2011): 223–56, doi:10.1111/j.1469-8129.2011.00491.x.

22 K. V. Korostelina, *Social Identity and Conflict: Structure, Dynamics and Implications* (New York: Palgrave Macmillan, 2007).

23 P. Connor, "More Than Nine-in-Ten People Worldwide Live in Countries with Travel Restrictions Amid COVID-19," 2020, accessed June 13, 2020, www.pewresearch.org/fact-tank/2020/04/01/more-than-nine-in-ten-people-world wide-live-in-countries-with-travel-restrictions-amid-COVID-19/.

24 John Allen et al., "How the World Will Look After the Coronavirus Pandemic," *Foreign Policy*, March 20, 2020, accessed June 14, 2020, https://foreignpolicy.com/2020/03/20/world-order-after-coroanvirus-pandemic/.

25 J. M. Krogstad and M. H. Lopez, "Americans Favor Medical Care but Not Economic Aid for Undocumented Immigrants Affected by COVID-19," 2020, accessed June 14, 2020, www.pewresearch.org/fact-tank/2020/05/20/americans-favor-medical-care-but-not-economic-aid-for-undocumented-immigrants-affected-by-COVID-19/.

26 YouGov/Brunswick Group Survey Results, "Health Policy 200429," 2020, accessed June 15, 2020, https://docs.cdn.yougov.com/00lzyll3i0/BrunswickGroup_client_topline_website.pdf.

27 R. Youngs, "Coronavirus and Europe's New Political Fissures: Carnegie Europe," 2020, accessed June 11, 2020, https://carnegieeurope.eu/2020/06/10/coronavirus-and-europe-s-new-political-fissures-pub-82023?utm_source=carnegieemail&utm_medium=email&utm_campaign=announcement&mkt_tok=eyJpIjoiTkdRNE5tUTNNRE0wWWVdFeiIsInQiOiJYbU5jbmRtNV JBRUNLZThuZ2gzYlwvVUNINndpdDB6UUFzb0ZXRnFMczFHKzl WdHJQZm53Tm5vZFpLYzRWQXorZ3pqMnBsRXhJSE45ZWF0dFZLNzkw YU5mZExqK2JlYkpvvQnloZ1A5TkhZWU12a1IzcktzNU1NWkRMMdnJLMEp vdVQifQ%3D%3D.

28 T. Gebrekal, "What Worries the World: 13 of the 27 Surveyed Nations Cited COVID-19 as the Top Concern," *Ipsos*, 2020, accessed June 27, 2020, www.ipsos.com/en/what-worries-world-june-2020.

29 Associated Press, "Serbia Criticizes Montenegro for Keeping Border Ban on Serbs, VOA," 2020, accessed June 12, 2020, www.voanews.com/COVID-19-pandemic/serbia-criticizes-montenegro-keeping-border-ban-serbs.

30 Human Rights Watch, "COVID-19 Fueling Anti-Asian Racism and Xenophobia Worldwide," 2020, accessed June 11, 2020, www.hrw.org/news/2020/05/12/COVID-19-fueling-anti-asian-racism-and-xenophobia-worldwide.

31 CBP, "Illegal Alien Tests Positive for COVID-19. U.S. Customs and Border Protection," 2020, accessed June 14, 2020, www.cbp.gov/newsroom/speeches-and-statements/illegal-alien-tests-positive-COVID-19.

32 M. Hackman, "Trump Moves to Temporarily Suspend New H-1B, Other Visas Amid Covid-19 Pandemic," *The Wall Street Journal*, June 23, 2020. www.wsj.com/articles/trump-order-would-temporarily-suspend-new-h-1b-other-visas-11592853371.

33 J. E. Stiglitz, *Globalization and Its Discontents Revisited: Anti-Globalization in the Era of Trump* (New York: W.W. Norton, 2017).

References

Afkhami, A. A. *Iran in the Age of Epidemics. Nationalism and the Struggle tor Public Health: 1889–1926*. New Haven: Yale University Press, 2003.

Mudde, Cas, and Cristóbal Rovira Kaltwasser. *Populism: A Very Short Introduction*. 2nd ed. New York: Oxford University Press, 2017.

7 A new global covenant?

Great power conflicts and conflict resolution in the post-corona era

Mohammed Cherkaoui

A lively debate has already begun about the potential effects of the current crisis and coming period of recovery on the global political order. One school of thought emphasizes a shift in the global balance of power toward the Asian nations that demonstrated their ability to deal with collective threats while the West proved less able to do so. Others predict a resurgence of European solidarity and social democracy, while still others foresee an accelerated trend toward nationalist isolation. The possibility of intensified competition between Great Powers is generating discussion about the need for UN reform and the creation of new conflict resolution facilities. This chapter describes key elements of the international agenda post-corona and suggests opportunities for significant peacemaking.

The coronavirus era indicates deep, if yet unmeasured, shifts in how the human race will reconstruct public health, science, economy, security, state power, and other variables of international relations. It also showcases a transitional period that indicates the rise and fall of certain international orders; however, it may represent the "tipping point from the international liberal order to disorder" (Tocci, 2020).[1] Future historians might well reflect back on two distant eras: BC (before coronavirus) and AC (after Coronavirus). A coronavirus-driven transition between BC and AC could be much deeper than the previous mega turns in history such as Globalization in the 1980s; end of Colonialism in the 1960s; Feudalism in the 1900s; Modernity starting in the 1850s; and the Industrial Revolution in the fifteenth century. As for the coronavirus trajectory, most observers are skeptical since "the signs are not promising that the major powers either comprehend the risks of the current transitional period or have a clear vision for a new international order that would be broadly acceptable and thus considered legitimate by most other states" (Stares, 2020).[2]

This chapter examines the potential effects of the current crisis and coming period of recovery on the global political order, and foresees four potential structural shifts. There has been a split of opinions: one school of thought emphasizes a shift in the global balance of power toward the Asian nations that demonstrated their ability to deal with collective threats while the West proved less able to do so. Qingguo Jia, Dean of the School of International Studies at Peking University, maintains the post-World War II order is not ending but is clearly in "serious trouble."[3] Others predict a resurgence of European solidarity and social democracy, while still others foresee an accelerated trend toward nationalist isolation. Some Europe enthusiasts notice Chancellor Angela Merkel's handling of the pandemic has given the opportunity "to assert her leadership on the international scene" (Bas, 2020).[4] The possibility of intensified competition between Great Powers is generating discussion about the need for U.N. reform and the creation of new conflict resolution facilities. What does the international agenda look like post-corona? What opportunities for significant peacemaking are likely to appear?

The Thucydides Trap, Europe Über Alles, and a Sectarian Cold War

The coronavirus moment has been a test of medical capacity and of political will as well, both in national and international terms. It would strengthen states, reinforce nationalisms and closed-door policies, and ultimately undermine globalism. Hal Brands, the Henry Kissinger Distinguished Professor at Johns Hopkins University's School of Advanced International Studies, points to an ironic lesson: we are not once again on the brink of global war, "not every crisis is the 1930s all over again. But conflict and rivalry are endemic to international affairs, and we forget that at our peril" (Brands, 2020).[5]

China has positioned itself to be the "doctor and the lab" of the West in 2020. President Xi described his country's medical assistance for Europe as an effort to further a "Health Silk Road," stretching his Belt and Road trade-and-infrastructure initiative. However, Chinese officials have been criticized for mounting a "propaganda campaign" to make certain Western states look like the Three Stooges. The new pandemic has only accelerated a west-to-east shift of power. President Trump's condemnation of the World Health Organization (WHO) for siding with Beijing was an indicator of a world disorder despite the short-lived "mask diplomacy" (Hornung, 2020).[6]

Political realism scholars, like Stephen Walt and Francis Fukuyama, agree on this easternization of the global distribution of power; "South Korea and Singapore have responded best, and China has reacted well after its early mistakes. The response in Europe and America has been slow and haphazard by comparison, further tarnishing the aura of the Western 'brand'" (Walt, 2020).[7] However, soft power theorist Joseph Nye argues coronavirus will not change the global order, and the pandemic is "unlikely to prove a geopolitical turning point." He also maintains "while the United States will continue to hold most of the high cards, misguided policy decisions could cause it to play these cards poorly" (Nye, 2020)[8]

China remains determined to challenge what it perceives as a "West-centric" existing global order. It also intends to capitalize on the withdrawal of the Trump administration from several international organizations, including UNESCO, the Paris Agreement on climate change, the Universal Postal Union, the Joint Comprehensive Plan of Action, and also Trump's criticism of NATO and his new feud with the International Criminal Court (ICC). Chinese officials perceive the Trump administration's policies as "an exception rather than the rule in post – World War II U.S. activities" (Jia, 2020).[9] They will not seek a direct clash with the United States or sleepwalk into a Thucydides's trap, which assumes all rising powers inevitably clash with the predominant powers (Allison, 2017).[10] Instead, China will remain eager to patiently watch the continued decline of the United States' standing in the world, while most countries have opted to remain active members in those institutions and pacts.

By late March 2020, the science of coronavirus turned into a battle of knowledge, brain drain, and Trumpian profiteering. The German government expressed resentment to the news that President Trump had offered $1bn to the Tübingen-based biopharmaceutical company, CureVac, to secure the vaccine "only for the United States."[11] German economy minister Peter Altmaier pointedly stated "Germany is not for sale." His colleague foreign minister Heiko Maas asserted "German researchers are taking a leading role in developing medication and vaccines as part of global cooperation networks. We cannot allow a situation where others want to exclusively acquire the results of their research."[12]

Chancellor Merkel was described as a leader who "maintained an open democracy in times of crisis." Her March 18 address to the nation was well-received and brought her more admiration. The influential *Sueddeutsche Zeitung* newspaper wrote, "Merkel painted a picture of the greatest challenge since World War II, but she did not speak of war . . . She did not rely on martial words or gestures, but on people's reason. . . . Nobody knows if that will be enough, but her tone will at least not lead the people to sink into uncertainty and fear."[13] She is the only world leader who included in her team social scientists and experts in constitutional rights to help plan the transition into a post-coronavirus era. Germans found "Mutti," the affectionate nickname they had been using for years; "a Mutti whose management of the crisis with scientific rigor, empathy and pragmatism has stood in stark contrast to the erratic, dramatic and chaotic management of many leaders."[14] Merkel's leadership has also made headlines after she hosted the

56th Munich Security Conference, and earlier the Conference on Peace in Libya on the 19th of January in Berlin, under a provocative title of "Westlessness," which refers to a world without Western dominance.

A third significant geopolitical shift is the deepening uncertainty, rise of nationalisms in the Middle East, and the Turkish–Iranian–Israeli–Saudi–Emirati power showdown. These regional hegemonic projects in Syria, Yemen, and Libya add to the blurry post-coronavirus reality, and Ian Bremmer's notion of a "G-Zero world" and a "geopolitical recession."[15] For instance, Iran turned down the U.S. offer of assistance by loosening sanctions on the Iranian banking system. Iran's foreign ministry spokesman Abbas Mousavi denounced Pompeo's offer as "a ridiculous claim and a political and psychological play" and condemned United States "economic terrorism."[16]

Israeli plans of annexing parts of the occupied West Bank have already sent signals of a hot summer of boiling tensions. Israel's Prime Minister Benjamin Netanyahu has vowed to annex up to 30% of the West Bank by July 1, and said the move, stemming from President Trump's peace plan, will write another "glorious chapter in the history of Zionism."[17] The annexation plan adds to the complexity of the Israel–Palestinian conflict and raises questions about the Palestinians' rights of existence on a map that has been described as resembling "Swiss cheese."

The coronavirus era will also accelerate the rise of new silos of power as symmetrical three-tier groupings of states: a superpower, a regional power, and small states. For instance, several Middle East countries have repositioned themselves around these silos of power: The United States, Israel, Egypt, Saudi Arabia, United Arab Emirates vis-a-vis Russia, Iran, Turkey, and Qatar. Russia has intervened politically and militarily in Syria and established two major bases: Hmeimim Air Base in the south-east of the city of Latakia, sharing some airfield facilities with Bassel Al-Assad International Airport; and the naval facility which Moscow considers as "Material-Technical Support Point" on the northern edge of the seaport of the Syrian city of Tartus.

The June 5, 2017, blockade of Qatar by the Quartet (Saudi Arabia, UAE, Bahrain, and Egypt) has strengthened Doha's trade, military, and diplomatic ties with Turkey and Iran. I was invited to Doha in May 2018 to make a presentation entitled "*A Geopolitical Outlook of the Gulf Crisis Trajectory: Political and Strategic Variables,*" while considering the region could become a tinderbox of tensions under Trump's unsettled policy toward Iran and Saudi Arabia and how any United States–Iran standoff would be a catalyst of future developments. I foresaw three main variables: a) strength of a Saudi–UAE–American–Israeli axis as a major realignment of U.S. strategic relationships in the region; b) Saudi Arabia would bear embarrassment in

Yemen and targeted by missile attacks launched by the Houthis across the border; and c) the Saudi and Emirati money will exhaust its potential in generating political capital in Washington.

The repetitive attacks on oil tankers in the Gulf in 2019 provided an opportunity for the Kremlin to present its "Russia's Security Concept for the Gulf Area" as a "collective" plan of action. The Russian Mission at the United Nations delivered a letter to the Security Council and the General Assembly July 23, 2019, arguing that the idea of establishing a security system in the Gulf area "might be essential for consolidating political and diplomatic efforts in this region. It implies a long-term program of action aimed at normalizing the situation, improving stability and security, resolving conflicts, identifying key benchmarks and parameters for a future postcrisis architecture, as well as ways to fulfill the related tasks."[18] Three months later, China decided to support the Russian plan, and maximize its potential in replacing the Gulf's US defense umbrella, and position Russia as "a power broker alongside the US," amid heightened tensions as a result of "tit-for-tat tanker seizures and a beefed-up US and British military presence in Gulf waters."[19]

Pandemic deterrence and human dimension in a post-U.N. World?

The WHO was reluctant to announce that the coronavirus was "officially a pandemic" and did not decide to bring the bad news until March 11. Dr. Ghebreyesus stated, "There is so much attention to that word. Other words matter more: prevention, preparedness, political leadership and people . . . We're in this together."[20] Months later, coronavirus has infected tens of millions of individuals and millions of deaths. The fluctuations of the coronavirus infection rate and death toll have challenged national governments and the United Nations system alike. Two revealing statements in New York and Geneva showcase not the devastating impact of the pandemic only, but also the inability of the existing world order to act. U.N. Secretary-General António Guterres believes the pandemic exposed "tremendous shortcomings, fragilities and fault lines."[21] In Geneva, the best advice suggested by Dr. Ghebreyesus was as follows: "please quarantine politicizing COVID. We shouldn't waste time pointing fingers."[22]

World diplomats at the U.N. headquarters in New York and public health experts at the WHO in Geneva have been bewildered in responding to a global raison-d'être tough question. Two recent resolution drafts presented at the Security Council, one by France and Tunisia, and the other by Germany and Estonia, call for a "humanitarian pause for at least 90 consecutive days" in order to allow for the delivery of aid to the hardest-hit communities.[23] However, the Trump administration has threatened to use its veto if there were any explicit reference to the WHO, which Trump has accused of downplaying the seriousness of the virus outbreak that began in China. He also notified the U.N. Secretary General of the U.S. withdrawal from the WHO effective July 6, 2021. This decision has been considered to be "among the most ruinous presidential decisions in recent history," and it would "make Americans less safe during an unprecedented global health crisis," as argued Lawrence O. Gostin, director of Georgetown University's O'Neill Institute for National and Global Health Law.[24]

As an uncontrollable cross-border pandemic, coronavirus is a new harrowing reminder of the fragility of human life and will deepen a public health-centered BC/AC historical periodization. French Doctor and virologist microbiologist, Didier Raoult, told French legislators in Paris the battle with Coronavirus has been "70 to 80 percent politics and 20 to 30 percent science." He also exposed some lobbyists against the use of Hydroxychloroquine, which he considers "the least expensive and simplest way to treat the coronavirus." The BC-AC transition may not lead to abolishing the WHO and replacing the United Nations; however, the coronavirus aftermath will be paving the way for three possible scenarios:

First, there will be a renewed debate about the Security Council reform in light of the 2005 deliberation at the General Assembly. Brazil's representative, one of the Group of Four (G-4 besides Japan, Germany, and India), who were aspiring to become permanent members of the Council, stated "the realities of power of 1945 had long been superseded. The security structure established then was now glaringly outdated."[25] Japan's ambassador asserted "countries with the will and resources to play a major role in international peace and security must always take part in the Council's decision-making process."[26] Now, the fear of coronavirus may lead to short-term isolationism. However, the conventional wisdom will restore the significance of international cooperation by necessity in the long term; and there could be a silver lining in the transition out of this gloomy coronavirus cave to reconstruct the U.N. system.

In the Declaration on the Commemoration of the *Seventy-Fifth Anniversary of the United Nations* to be released on September 21, 2020, diplomats in New York seem to have internalized a sense of unfounded praise and claim of "owning" the discourse of peace. They argue "there is no other global organization with the legitimacy, convening power and normative impact as the United Nations. No other global organization gives hope to so many people for a better world and can deliver the future we want."[27]

One may not contest the promise of the U.N. Charter and the normative foundation of the whole system, but coronavirus has called for some pragmatism and efficiency in delivery of the promised goals. Germany is well positioned to push once again for the U.N. reform and the way it operates and "laying the lasting foundations for a Globalization 2.0 in the interests of the greatest number of people."[28] There could be a "Merkel moment" to promote a new, fair, and balanced internationalism. The Enlightenment Kantian paradigm, which was significant in the creation of the League of Nations, and later the United Nations, may return to inspire the post-corona global politics with the focus on the individual, the free moral self and subject, placing structure and all the embedded political institutions and economic regulations at the periphery, with an open mind for perpetual peace. Kant urged the self to "act only on that maxim through which you can at the same time will that it should become a universal law."[29]

Second, there will be reluctant acceptance among Great Powers of a shift from nuclear deterrence to pandemic deterrence. One good indicator is the first NATO foreign ministerial by secure video teleconference April 2 where NATO's response occupied much of the agenda. NATO Secretary General Jens Stoltenberg observed that the coronavirus crisis was "too great for any one nation or organization to face alone."[30] In Washington, the Congressional Research Service raised the question of whether and how the global pandemic might lead to "profoundly transformative and long-lasting changes in the U.S. role in the world."[31] The existing 13,410 nuclear weapons in the world have not defeated the coronavirus attacks across the five continents. However, the Trump administration has reassured the new pandemic will not affect its nuclear weapon investments while allocating a 20% increase this year.

The existing balance of power inside the Security Council will be challenged by a coronavirus-shaped momentum at the General Assembly. For seventy-five years after WWII, humanity has been told nuclear weapons are "necessary and essential" for international security and strategic balance of power; and without them, the world would face another global conflict. Now, this nuclearism is waning and being marginalized by rising coronavirusim and its threat of a public health and economic apocalypse of the early 2020s.

Third, there will be prominence of the human dimension and ecological imperative in reconstructing the world order. Public health will gain significance in any conceptualization of national and international security. Any BC-to-AC historical periodization will strengthen the need for the pandemic deterrence, as an offshoot of the highly advocated basic human needs by the conflict resolution community, or the "human dimension" as theorized by Abraham Maslow and John Burton. The *Seventy-Fifth Anniversary of the United Nations* declaration indicates the General Assembly's "full support" for reviewing "the peacebuilding architecture."

The United Nations Development Program, the most nuanced organ of the U.N. system in dealing with the global socio-economic challenges, has constructed its coronavirus crisis response to help policymakers look beyond recovery, toward 2030, in four main areas: governance, social protection, green economy, and digital disruption.[32] U.N. Chief Guterres also believes the impact of coronavirus "is adding fuel to an already burning fire of discontent and anxiety."[33] He has called for action on three fronts: a) immediate support for at-risk workers, enterprises, jobs, and incomes to avoid closures, job losses, and income decline; b) greater focus on both health and economic activity after lockdowns ease, with workplaces that are safe, and rights for women and populations at risk; and c) we need to mobilize now for a human-centered, green and sustainable, inclusive recovery that harnesses the potential of new technologies to create decent jobs for all – and draws on the creative and positive ways companies and workers have adapted to these times.[34] Guterres's three recommendations echo the need for gratifying basic human needs. They also make a hint of a strategic shift from power to public health and economic survival as a new unit of analysis.

Notes

1 Nathalie Tocci, "The European Union," in *Perspectives on a Changing World Order*, ed. Paul B. Stares et al., Discussion Paper Series on Managing Global Disorder No. 1 (New York: Council on Foreign Relations, June 2020).

2 Paul B. Stares et al., eds., *Perspectives on a Changing World Order*, Discussion Paper Series on Managing Global Disorder No. 1 (New York: Council on Foreign Relations, June 2020).

3 Qingguo Jia, "China," in *Perspectives on a Changing World Order*, ed. Paul B. Stares et al., Discussion Paper Series on Managing Global Disorder No. 1 (New York: Council on Foreign Relations, June 2020).

4 Jean-Christophe Bas, "Promoting a New Balanced Internationalism: The 'Merkel Moment'?," *Dialogue of Civilizations Research Institute*, June 3, 2020, https://doc-research.org/2020/06/promoting-new-balanced-internationalism-merkel-moment/.

5 Hal Brands, "Coronavirus Hasn't Killed the Global Balance of Power," *The Japan Times*, May 31, 2020, www.japantimes.co.jp/opinion/2020/05/31/commentary/world-commentary/coronavirus-hasnt-killed-global-balance-power/#.XvB3imgzZPY.

6 Jeffrey W. Hornung, "Don't Be Fooled by China's Mask Diplomacy," *RAND Corporation*, May 5, 2020, www.rand.org/blog/2020/05/dont-be-fooled-by-chinas-mask-diplomacy.html.

7 Stephen Walt et al., "How the World Will Look After the Coronavirus Pandemic," *Foreign Policy*, March 20, 2020, https://foreignpolicy.com/2020/03/20/world-order-after-coroanvirus-pandemic/.

8 Joseph Nye, "No, the Coronavirus Will Not Change the Global Order," *Foreign Policy*, April 16, 2020, https://foreignpolicy.com/2020/04/16/coronavirus-pandemic-china-united-states-power-competition/.

9 Jia, "China."

10 Graham Allison, *Destined for War: Can America and China Escape Thucydides' Trap?* (New York: Houghton Mifflin Harcourt, 2017).

11 "Coronavirus: Anger in Germany at Report Trump Seeking Exclusive Vaccine Deal," *The Guardian*, March 16, 2020, www.theguardian.com/world/2020/mar/16/not-for-sale-anger-in-germany-at-report-trump-seeking-exclusive-coronavirus-vaccine-deal.

12 Ibid.

13 France 24, "Merkel Shines in Handling of Germany's Coronavirus Crisis," March 29, 2020, www.france24.com/en/20200329-merkel-shines-in-handling-of-germany-s-coronavirus-crisis.

14 Bas, "Promoting a New Balanced Internationalism."

15 Ian Bremmer, "We Are in a Geopolitical Recession: That's a Bad Time for the Global Coronavirus Crisis," *Time*, March 13, 2020, https://time.com/5802033/geopolitical-recession-global-crisis/.

16 Matthew Petti, "Coronavirus: The Deadly New U.S.-Iran Standoff," *The National Interest*, March 9, 2020, https://nationalinterest.org/blog/middle-east-watch/coronavirus-deadly-new-us-iran-standoff-131197.

17 Tom Bateman, "Israel Annexation: New Border Plans Leave Palestinians in Despair," *BBC*, June 25, 2005, www.bbc.com/news/world-middle-east-53139808.

18 The Russian Ministry of Foreign Affairs, "Russia's Security Concept for the Gulf Area," July 23, 2019, www.mid.ru/en/liga-arabskih-gosudarstv-lag-/-/asset_publisher/0vP3hQoCPRg5/content/id/3733593.

19 James M. Dorsey, "Will There Be a New Russian-Chinese Security Architecture in the Gulf?" *BESA*, September 13, 2019, https://besacenter.org/perspectives-papers/russia-china-security-gulf/.

20 World Economic Forum, "Coronavirus Is Officially a Pandemic – but We Can Change Its Course: Today's WHO Briefing," March 11, 2020, www.weforum.org/agenda/2020/03/coronavirus-is-official-a-pandemic-but-we-can-change-its-course-who-briefing/.

21 António Guterres, "Launch of Policy Brief on COVID-19 and the World of Work," *UN News*, www.un.org/en/coronavirus/world-work-cannot-and-should-not-look-same-after-crisis.

22 UN News, "No Need to Politicize COVID-19: UN Health Agency Chief," April 8, 2020, https://news.un.org/en/story/2020/04/1061392.

23 "New Resolution on Immediate Global Ceasefire Presented to UN Security Council," *AFP*, May 13, 2020, www.france24.com/en/20200513-new-resolution-on-global-ceasefire-during-covid-19-pandemic-presented-to-un-security-council.

24 Katie Rogers and Apoorva Mandavilli, "Trump Administration Signals Formal Withdrawal from W.H.O.," *The New York Times*, July 7, 2020, www.nytimes.com/2020/07/07/us/politics/coronavirus-trump-who.html.

25 United Nations General Assembly, "General Assembly Opens Debate on 'Group of Four'-Sponsored Draft Resolution on Security Council Reform," July 11, 2005, GA/10367, www.un.org/press/en/2005/ga10367.doc.htm.

26 Ibid.

27 General Assembly of the United Nations, "75th Anniversary of UN," June 5, 2020, www.un.org/pga/74/2020/06/05/75th-anniversary-of-un/.

28 Bas, "Promoting a New Balanced Internationalism."

29 Immanuel Kant, *Groundwork of the Metaphysics of Morals*, trans. Jonathan F. Bennett, www.earlymoderntexts.com/pdf/kantgw.pdf.

30 Rachel Ellehuus, "NATO Responds to the Covid-19 Pandemic," *CSIS*, April 2, 2020, www.csis.org/analysis/nato-responds-covid-19-pandemic.

31 Congressional Research Service, "U.S. Role in the World: Background and Issues for Congress," *Atlantic*, June 22, 2020.

32 UNDP, "COVID-19 Pandemic Humanity Needs Leadership and Solidarity to Defeat the Coronavirus," www.undp.org/content/undp/en/home/coronavirus.html.

33 Guterres, "Launch of Policy Brief on COVID-19 and the World of Work."

34 Ibid.

Part III

Intergroup conflicts after the pandemic

8 The triple crisis

Reevaluating socio-economic values in a period of social reconstruction

Michael D. English

The combined biomedical and economic crises of 2020 threw the spotlight on inequalities of class, status, and opportunity that had been growing rapidly for several decades. This essay argues that the desires of some groups to return to "normalcy" after the pandemic are likely to be overwhelmed by long-repressed cravings for system change aimed at re-prioritizing social ethics. This situation poses dangers to peace, but also significant opportunities for constructive action. Conflict specialists can contribute to the nonviolent transformation of a system that has long sanctified inequality. Among other contributions, they can assist movements seeking social justice to adopt a spirit of respect for individual rights and cultural differences.

Introduction

A crisis is not the root cause of any particular problem, but rather the visible manifestation of internal contradictions within a given system that can no longer be regulated through existing conflict management mechanisms. At the current time, much of the world is experiencing three crises: a global pandemic caused by the coronavirus, a severe economic downturn, and mass protests against racial and ethnic inequities. These crises, it seems clear, are intertwined and deeply rooted in the social structures and relations of the global capitalist system. As time passes, it appears increasingly unlikely that the post-coronavirus world will return to the status quo ante. If, as some commentators argue, the world is being changed in significant ways, what does that change look like, and what role will this triple crisis play in creating new socio-economic values to guide post-pandemic society?

Let us not forget that the period of economic recovery following the Great Recession was also a decade of intense activism targeting issues of political marginalization, economic inequality, and systemic racism. We saw the emergence of numerous local and transnational movements dedicated to achieving social, political, and economic justice, including the Arab Spring,

Occupy Wall Street, Umbrella Revolution, and Black Lives Matter. Analysts have pointed out that the circumstances most favorable to mass mobilizations for change postcrisis feature economic growth rather than collapse and rising rather than falling group expectations.[1] Stearns and Rubenstein (Chapter 2) argue a suggestive analogy is the period of the Great Depression, when a highly uneven recovery taking place in an environment of mass activism provided the basis for a wave of historic political and social reforms in the United States and Western Europe. The grievances underpinning the movements that erupted in the 2010s emerged during a period of rising economic growth and rising expectations. They are foundational for the contemporary struggles playing out presently. Yet these movements also emerged at a time when a number of states were turning away from liberal democratic norms to embrace nationalist, authoritarian-oriented regimes. Demands for justice are increasingly contrasted with isolationist and xenophobic policies designed to pull states away from the postwar liberal consensus rather than further it. As such, an analysis of the triple crisis is necessary to demonstrate what those interested in transcending the internal contradictions of the present system must consider, and the potential for liberal, nationalist, and socially radical responses to constitute or reconstitute social, economic, and political norms in the future.

The triple crisis

The first crisis appeared in the form of a biomedical global pandemic. The novel coronavirus or COVID-19 is a highly infectious illness capable of being transmitted person-to-person via symptomatic and asymptomatic carriers; it is decidedly more deadly than the common flu. In response, governments across the world took the unprecedented step of initiating lockdown measures to control the movement of populations and limit foreign visitors. The severity of measures varied by country, but by March 2020, much of the world's population was in isolation. Health officials presented the decision to quarantine people in their homes, in some cases for months, as the most appropriate form of action. Once Seattle and New York City became hot spots, even a reluctant President Trump deferred to the guidance of health experts.

Yet, the lockdown measures quickly produced a second crisis. By April, the global economy had ground to halt. Commercial airlines, the bastions of liberal globalization and a means by which COVID-19 spread, were the first to feel the blow as temporarily canceled flights became permanent. The majority of businesses, government agencies, and schools closed. Unemployment rates soared as employers laid off and furloughed workers in an effort to shield themselves from the fiscal impacts. The International

Monetary Fund noted this was the "Worst Economic Downturn Since the Great Depression."[2] In under four months, an isolated biomedical crisis went global, triggering an economic crisis, and erasing a decade of recovery. Millions were now unemployed and in need of financial assistance, and essential goods such as personal protective equipment and toilet paper were suddenly scarce.

That the lockdowns had such quick and devastating consequences for today's globalized capitalist system is unsurprising. Capital requires constant circulation to function and generate value.[3] Given the interconnectedness of the global economy, when circulation stops, especially in countries such as China and the United States, the effects are bound to be immediate and profound. Both production and consumption are drastically curtailed, thus requiring government intervention to stabilize the purportedly self-regulating market system. The preference to prioritize the economy over the health of the population rapidly became clear. The US government gave trillions in bailouts for corporations and Wall Street, yet members of Congress agonized over the distribution of $1200 stimulus payments to workers fearing they would encourage laborers not to return to work. Nor would the government commit to covering all costs associated with testing, treating, and preventing COVID-19. While hospital workers pleaded for necessary protective gear, the state took a hands-off approach, insisting the market decide how supplies were manufactured and distributed. In undercutting health officials, Trump's new mantra, "The cure cannot be worse than the problem," summed-up a growing consensus among shareholders, financiers, merchants, and a small segment of workers that mass public death was an acceptable risk for saving the economy.

Surprisingly, the first public demonstrations came not as a response to the state's failure to address the severity of COVID-19 or the scant economic support for the public. Instead, a coalition of conservative-libertarian groups upset about the lockdowns emerged, framing the crisis in terms of government tyranny – officials were deploying quarantine measures to suppress individual liberty. These mostly white actors gathered at state capitals in armed convoys, occasionally occupying government buildings, and largely ignoring social distancing and facial covering requirements to prevent COVID-19's spread. Reaction to these demonstrations spilt along partisan lines. The Left ridiculed the banality of the protestors' messages (i.e., "I want a haircut"), their heavily militarized appearance (e.g., AR-15s and camouflage outfits), as well as the unwillingness of police to enforce public health orders. The Right offered encouragement, echoing their support for opening the economy and challenging government overreach, while also voicing minor criticism that protestors were making gun owners look bad and utilizing protest tactics associated with the Left.

The biomedical and economic crises amplified existing trends in economic inequality, racial disparities, and existing political divisions. As the number of positive cases and deaths grew, the distribution of suffering from the virus mirrored the distribution of those already existing in precarious conditions – poor communities and communities of color were affected with higher rates of hospitalizations, mortality, and with more economic consequences.[4] Epidemiologists expressed that the illness cared little in terms of who it infected; nevertheless, their message misrepresented the degree of suffering faced by different communities.

The methods necessary to prevent the spread of COVID-19 – social distancing and quarantine – decidedly affected laborers in low-wage jobs now considered essential, communities without access to adequate health care, and persons living in situations where quarantining was impossible. Charles M. Blow, of *The New York Times*, captured the paradox for those trapped in a no-win situation:

> *Staying at home is a privilege. Social distancing is a privilege. The people who can't must make terrible choices: Stay home and risk starvation or go to work and risk contagion . . . Our entire discussion around this virus is stained with economic elitism . . . people chastise black and brown people for not always being inside, but many of those doing the chastising do so from comfortable homes with sufficient money and food.*[5]

While commentators effectively turned the conversation to include race and economic inequality, the realization of these disparities alone did not call masses of people into the streets. A third crisis, political in nature, emerged in May due to the deaths of three African-Americans at the hands of police or former law enforcement. The murders of Ahmaud Arbery, Breonna Taylor, and George Floyd pushed systemic racism to the fore. Massive demonstrations erupted across the United States and around the globe drawing hundreds of thousands of participants to demand justice and police accountability. Police overreaction to the protests, particularly the heavy-handed use of militarized tactics including tear gas, rubber bullets, and mass corralling only furthered calls for police reform and abolition. The United States and many former European colonial powers find themselves immersed in conversations about social injustice and centuries of violence directed at people of color.

The triple crisis revealed unresolved tensions at the heart of the current liberal order. COVID-19 is a brutal reminder that humans remain members of the same species; nature does not discriminate based on political preferences or cultural differences – people do. The crisis exposed how systemic inequities within the existing order play a critical role in determining one's experiences and life chances. It also revealed the harmful consequences of decades of austerity policies (e.g., privatization of social services, removal of protections for workers, and offshoring manufacturing) and inability of the market to act as a replacement for the state. Finally, it presented a vivid reminder that the foundations of capitalism and modern policing are built on slavery, genocide, and institutionalized racism.[6]

Three visions of the future

As we consider the future postcrisis, we must address what Fraser (2013) describes as three distinct yet interrelated struggles for redistribution (inequality), recognition (identity), and representation (political inclusion).[7] The triple crisis demands a reconsideration of each of these areas as part of any transition out of the neoliberal present. For conflict intervenors in particular, the future raises the specter that any attempt to remain neutral is to misunderstand the nature of contemporary struggles and thus be irrelevant (at best) or complicit (at worst).

The triple crisis produced a number of reactions, but each of these fits an existing form that might be described as liberal, nationalist, or socially radical. The liberal form, in my view, remains the most untenable. Liberals hope for a postcrisis return to the status quo with political reforms aimed at mitigating some inequalities without significant system change. Rather than identify COVID-19 as a public health emergency demanding social solidarity, liberals label the virus as an occasion for "disruptors" to collaborate in public–private partnerships. More substantive attention will very likely be given to recognition, already visible in the vast corporate outpouring of support for racial justice. Liberals have no problem demanding reform of policing institutions since many of their persuasion view systemic racism to mean biased police officers.

The primary deficiency of the liberal perspective is that it does not deal with the underlying systemic factors generating or exacerbating the crisis. Instead, the triple crisis demonstrates that accumulation at the top remains pervasive – tech billionaires increased their wealth by billions in less than six months[8] – while those at the bottom struggle to maintain what they have, let alone return to pre-crisis standards. In terms of recognition, the fixation on individual bias leaves untouched the underlying purpose of modern policing, which remains committed to protecting private property and monitoring minority and low-income communities.[9]

In contrast, the nationalist resurgence of the past decade stands to benefit the most from the triple crisis (see Karina V. Korostelina's chapter in this volume). Here, the question of redistribution is taken seriously, even if the actions that flow from it are offensive (i.e., targeting foreigners and internal enemies). What the nationalist offers, especially those contemplating the fascist or neo-fascist route, is clarity. They accept that the economic system is broken – the nation is suffering as a result of misguided economic and social policies that benefit others, but not us.[10] The solution is not to transform the economic system but to demonize immigrants and the "criminal classes" as thieves and make it a people issue rather than a distribution issue. Nationalists have little concern with recognition, since, in their view, multiculturalism is also part of the problem. Hence, their unwillingness to acknowledge systemic racism and their tendency to blame victims of police violence for bringing it on themselves. Very specific policies flow from this perspective: 1) a continued focus on law and order, 2) promotion of essential national industries, 3) decreased protections for labor, and 4) further militarization. The nationalist vision for the future is one of violent conflict, both at home and abroad. National self-interest will not cure the current malaise though it may ultimately advantage richer nations over poorer ones.

Liberals, in their rush to chastise the anti-lockdown supporters as dupes of Trump, ignored that many participants were workers and small business owners – people directly affected by the economic crisis and receiving minimal government support. Liberals do not recognize how their own lack of solutions for reducing economic inequality sound to those who have only marginally benefited from the previous economic recovery. The nationalist appreciates that the fear of sliding back down the economic ladder is a powerful motivator and one that can easily be connected to anxieties over cultural preservation and diminished social status.

The social radical acknowledges the complexity of the inherent contradictions embedded in these systems, yet faces the difficult task of coordinating and sustaining movements for change. The challenge is intensified by continuing disagreement among social radicals over the prioritization of identity or inequality; those who favor identity emphasize marginalization due to race and gender, whereas those concerned with inequality emphasize the class dimension. On the surface, these differences do not seem that far apart, but they have proven divisive in practice. Simmons (2020) indicates that part of the tension is related to the different root narratives that inform and sustain each of these struggles.[11] In locating their grievance in identity or class, each group tells a similar but ultimately unique story about the nature of the problem and its potential solutions. The triple crisis presents radicals with the prospect of generating a new narrative that makes clear that the path forward must resolve both systemic racism and economic inequality and must do so in a manner that inspires mass political participation.

If social radicals are dedicated to systemic transformation, they must insist on a new set of postcapitalist values rooted in cooperative forms of economic and social justice as the foundations of a new social contract. This vision reimagines what it means to be part of the human community and the rights to which all are entitled. Such values appreciate their origins in the radical spirit of the Enlightenment, yet, aim to fulfill in deed what liberals committed to only in word. These values must support the primary task of seizing political power and using it to replace the existing neoliberal system with one that can address social inequities, meet basic needs, ensure justice and political inclusion. Action taken by radicals to address the underlying causes of the triple crisis may yield an increase in social conflict in the near future, yet such struggles remain vital. The Right's re-embrace of fascism shows there is no arc of history toward justice; the fight for justice is continual and it is ours to lose.

To achieve these ends, social radicals will have to overcome their fear of state power; they can no longer cede control of the state to nationalists and capitalists. The rise of neofascism and the coming environmental collapse makes the state an essential site of struggle. Radicals must increase mass participation in elections and win decisive victories to legitimize their policies. They must deploy state power to provide for populations and protect them from biological, ecological, and economic disasters, as well as from abuses of power. Additionally, they must direct state institutions to produce goods, deliver services, and enforce policies that mutual aid alone is not suited for and the free market unwilling to provide – such as developing and distributing a free vaccine for COVID-19. Overcoming systemic racism means not only demilitarizing police forces and prison abolition but also envisioning and institutionalizing new forms of community safety that prioritize treatment and restoration. Moreover, this requires a drastic reduction in military expenditures and the military's role as a means of international diplomacy.

Notes

1 Ted Robert Gurr, *Why Men Rebel* (Princeton, NJ: Princeton University Press, 1971).
2 Gita Gopinath, "The Great Lockdown: Worst Economic Downturn Since the Great Depression," *IMF Blog*, April 14, 2020, https://blogs.imf.org/2020/04/14/the-great-lockdown-worst-economic-downturn-since-the-great-depression/.
3 David Harvey, *The Enigma of Capital: And the Crises of Capitalism* (Oxford: Oxford University Press, 2010).
4 Mark Hugo Lopez, Lee Rainie, and Abby Budiman, "Financial and Health Impacts of COVID-19 Vary Widely by Race and Ethnicity," *Pew Research Center*, May 5, 2020. www.pewresearch.org/fact-tank/2020/05/05/financial-and-health-impacts-of-covid-19-vary-widely-by-race-and-ethnicity/.
5 Charles M. Blow, "Social Distancing Is a Privilege," *The New York Times*, April 5, 2020, www.nytimes.com/2020/04/05/opinion/coronavirus-social-distancing.html.

6 Ta-Nehisi Coates, "The Case for Reparations," *The Atlantic*, June 2014; Angela Y. Davis, *Women, Race, & Class* (New York: Vintage, 1983).

7 Nancy Fraser, *Fortunes of Feminism* (New York: Verso, 2013).

8 Jade Scipioni, "These 7 Billionaires' Net Worth Is Up More Than 50% Since Start of the Covid-19 Pandemic," *CNBC*, June 16, 2020, www.cnbc.com/2020/06/16/billionaires-net-worth-grew-amid-covid-19-pandemic-from-market-lows.html.

9 Alex S. Vitale, *The End of Policing* (London: Verso, 2017).

10 Jason Stanley, *How Fascism Works: The Politics of Us and Them* (New York: Random House, 2018).

11 Solon J. Simmons, *Root Narrative Theory and Conflict Resolution: Power, Justice and Values* (Abingdon, Oxon: Routledge, 2020).

9 Racial justice in a post-COVID America

Toward systemic conflict resolution and peacebuilding

Arthur Romano

There is overwhelming evidence that the COVID-19 epidemic struck African Americans, Latinxs, and other minorities in the U.S. far more severely than most white communities. Even Black citizens by police officers or former officers generated the largest demonstrations for racial justice since the heyday of the U.S. Civil Rights Movement. What is the likely future of this movement, and what will be its next stages of development? Will an uneven recovery from the medical and economic crises further exacerbate racial and ethnic struggles? This essay analyzes the causes of the wave of social unrest now agitating American society and discusses actions that conflict resolvers may take in the nonviolent pursuit of peace and justice.

In the United States, the COVID-19 pandemic has disproportionately killed and sickened racial minorities, especially African Americans. In Chicago, to give just one example, black individuals comprise more than 50% of COVID-19 cases and nearly 70% of COVID-19 deaths, although Blacks make up only 30% of the city's population. Moreover, these deaths are concentrated mostly in just five neighborhoods on Chicago's South Side (Yancy 2020).[1]

This dramatic racial disparity in COVID-19 outcomes shines a harsh spotlight on systemic racism and injustice in the United States. African Americans are more vulnerable to COVID-19 for a variety of reasons: They are more likely to live in areas segregated by race and poverty that have denser housing, intergenerational households, high crime rates, and poor access to healthy foods and basic health care. Blacks disproportionately struggle with comorbidities such as hypertension and obesity, which are all but inscriptions of the accumulated trauma of racism on their bodies (Guan et al. 2020).[2] Blacks are less likely to be able to telework (30% of Americans but fewer than 20% of Black and Latino workers) reported that they could do so before the pandemic (Gould and Shierholz 2020).[3] Many Black and Latino people hold low-wage, "essential" jobs that afford them almost no flexibility to work from the relative safety of home. They are running transportation systems, picking up garbage, ringing up groceries, working in high-risk healthcare settings such as nursing homes, and taking care of children.

Black people have long recognized and lived with these kinds of inequalities in housing, employment, health, and health care, but COVID-19 has made them visible for all to see. The pandemic had already revealed systemic racism when the tragic murder of George Floyd by a police officer in Milwaukee on May 25, 2020, unleashed public rage and anger against it. Large numbers of anti-racist protestors and sympathizers demanded a move away from incremental change and toward serious overhauls of a racially biased systems (most notably, policing). The size, spread, and frequency of these demonstrations took virtually all analysts by surprise, as did the appearance of a new generation of organizers and activists devoted to change. I believe that people will continue to take to the streets, join militant groups, inundate social media, and engage with increasing zeal in cultural change work and local experiments as social inequalities and the permanent underclass both grow.

For those interested in doing work related to conflicts of race in the United States, this situation poses dramatic new challenges. I want to argue here that the most immediate challenge for peacemakers is to join forces with racial justice movements and work to transform structural injustices, rather than focusing on conventional methods of "resolving" and "de-escalating" existing unrest. Many of the professional processes we imagine and promote are dialogue-based and take place within controlled settings with an underlying ethic of middle-class civility and a Habermasian aesthetic of how democratic social change occurs (Chilton and Wyant Cuzzo 2005).[4] In practice, however, people imagine and enact a democratic society in the messy and tenuous moments of wider unrest and civil resistance, as well as through everyday acts of resistance to injustice and local work aimed at constructing alternatives structures for meeting human needs (A. Y. Davis 2016; Escobar 2008; Lilja et al. 2017).[5] Productive conflict *escalation* is often an opportunity to promote deeper social change.

The debate between system maintenance and revolutionary work is certainly not a new one for our field; practitioners and scholars have been discussing these tensions for decades (Schoeny and Warfield 2000).[6] This moment, however, invites conflict practitioners to engage more extensively with questions of structural, systemically generated violence. For example, what would a just economic order in the United States and the world look like given the deeply entwined racist legacy of colonialism, slavery, and anti-immigrant movements that shaped American capitalism? How can democracy ensure the rights and well-being of all people, especially black people and other marginalized groups, when our political system was grounded in racial inequality from the start? More Americans are realizing that racism is not an issue solely of individual attitudes and good or bad intentions, but the result of intersecting systems that require change (Collins and Bilge 2020, Crenshaw 2017).[7] In June 2020, for example, over two million people participated in a Zoom call hosted by the Poor People's Campaign to learn more about how they could help address the intersecting issues of racism, poverty, and militarism.

This wider analytical awakening, while vital, does not automatically produce change, since powerful systems are often able to weather short-term unrest and reorganize themselves with superficial changes that leave broader patterns of oppression intact. Again, this suggests a creative role for peacebuilders and conflict resolution practitioners able to connect different activist networks. This engagement with advocates working across diverse domains, from rethinking criminal justice to transforming the economy and reimagining education, is challenging, since these individuals often have competing theories of change, employ diverse practices, and engage in varied organizational and professional cultures. A nonlinear and networked approach is needed when instigating systemic change, since shifts in understanding and new pathways for collaboration can influence change across multiple systems in ways that are hard to predict (Chesters 2004).[8] Meanwhile, social movements provide a large wave, or "outside" force, that exerts pressure on institutions, transforming what people think is possible in terms of justice in the society.

What does this kind of conflict resolution work – to advance systemic rather than piecemeal change – look like in practice? In part, it entails finding and supporting those activists who are already building bridges in their work. We can see the power of this kind of cross-pollination in the rich history of black women organizers from Harriet Tubman to Ella Baker (Gumbs 2014; Parker 2020).[9] It also exists with contemporary activist and peacebuilders such as the Black Lives Matter activists in Ferguson, Missouri, who connected with and formed alliances with other activists around the world, including Palestinians (Bailey 2015).[10] These leaders amplified their influence and incorporated greater complexity in their thinking by meeting policymakers and public intellectuals in the United States and abroad, including elder civil rights activists, professional athletes, and other public figures (Jackson and Foucault Welles 2016).[11] Over time, this approach mattered; during the uprisings following the deaths of George Floyd and Breonna Taylor, it helped shift the national conversation toward systemic solutions (e.g., how the system of policing works, and how police departments might be radically overhauled, decommissioned, defunded, or otherwise transformed).

Conflict resolution in and across networks requires specialized skills, including mapping and better understanding how knowledge circulates between and within varied political and social ecologies. Facilitating conversations about collaboration, ongoing conflicts, key impasses and differences in vision, entails moving beyond familiar constituencies and communities of practice and engaging with groups working in different or loosely connected domains. This ability to engage with greater complexity and build a broader and more diverse power base is a form of integrative power which is at the heart of networked conflict resolution (Boulding 1990).[12] Some of the work involves both horizontal and vertical exchange, or as Civil Rights Activist and pedagogue Dr. Bernard LaFayette puts it, "connecting the streets to the suites."

An important implication of this shift of focus for peace and conflict specialists is the need to develop our theories of change and learn more from practitioners about how systemic change actually occurs. This approach demands engaging with complexity on two major fronts: (a) understanding how to integrate change efforts across institutions and at different social levels; and (b) embracing and working with nonlinear and emergent dynamics in complex systems. Conflict scholar John Paul Lederach, for example, offers an alternative to focusing on "critical mass" by proposing the metaphor of "critical yeast" (Lederach 2005).[13] This phrase describes how a small number of influential actors can generate change like yeast making bread rise. Lederach's point is that *types* of connections are important, and not just the quantity ("critical mass") of people engaged. Even small changes across multiple networks can lead to tipping points, as systems are often interconnected and not as stable as we think. Mapping those systems, looking for new points of connection, and bolstering or creating new pathways and processes for exchange is key to work that seeks to catalyze the unpredictable.

Facilitating democratic engagement is a critical form of conflict resolution in order to engage growing numbers of people in influencing wider systemic change. For example, when it comes to uprooting police violence, policy change is critical to demilitarizing the police, creating a national database of police who have engaged in conduct violations, and limiting the power of police unions or dissolving them altogether. Furthermore, as many commentators have pointed out, major shifts in funding are needed to support community-based conflict resolution and stronger social services in areas affected by structural violence (Jenkins 2020).[14] But even this is not enough. We need economic policies that break down economic stratification and spatial segregation so that race, class, and one's ZIP code are no longer the largest determinants of one's access to quality jobs, health care, education, or protection from violence (including police violence).

Yet for peacebuilding to be effective over the long-term in addressing systemic racism actions have to emerge, as well, out of the knowledge and needs of local people and the leadership of Black people and other people of color. Solutions offered by experts and advanced by federal policies, however effective, are not enough. Although people frequently call for community engagement or culturally relevant perspectives, in reality violence prevention and urban education often rely heavily on expert-driven approaches (Ginwright 2010).[15] People of color living in America's most violence-affected cities are too often portrayed either as passive victims or irredeemable perpetrators of violence. This story neglects how people who live with these problems each day produce and share knowledge in their communities about the underlying causes of violence and how they might be addressed.

I believe that cities and the surrounding suburbs will present some of the best opportunities for systemic peacebuilding models with local and national implications. For conflict resolution practitioners committed to working within and between differing networks, the city provides the requisite complexity to help facilitate learning and advance broader collective action that can help connect these highly localized experiments with practices that build alternatives to systemic racism. For example, in urban communities, today peacebuilders engage in local truthtelling and restorative justice efforts and have created supportive spaces to work together to address police violence locally, and to join others nationally in the prevention of police violence (Romano and Ragland 2018).[16] Meanwhile, in schools, restorative justice has reduced suspensions and expulsions, kept people who would have gone to jail out of jail, and reduced recidivism (Brown 2019; González 2015; F. E. Davis, Lyubansky, and Schiff 2015).[17] Further activists have worked on developing Harm Free Zones similar to Zones of Peace, where conflict de-escalation practices, peace education, and restorative justice are used to create the conditions where community members can play a more active role in working for justice and rely less on police intervention (Herzing 2015).[18]

A systems approach to peacebuilding means supporting these movements, creating horizontal linkages between them, and building a diverse power base so that these grassroots efforts can be sustained and go to scale. In terms of integration, urban peacebuilding will increasingly facilitate hybrid forms of urban governance that connect grassroots and social movements with existing governance structures. For example, technological solutions like the app developed by Brandon Anderson Raheem helps communities report and track police behavior so that they can influence policy by directly through crowdsourcing efforts about police abuse of power (Gray 2020).[19] In Minneapolis, the city council is engaging community members to re-envision community safety, care, and support efforts as an alternative to militarized policing of communities of color (Solomon Gustavo 2020).[20] And in places like New Haven, Connecticut, activists and advocates are leading conflict de-escalation training for the police department in which they train police alongside community members in the philosophy and practice of nonviolence and critical reflection on systemic racism (Romano 2014).[21]

This is a painful and important moment in the United States as the convergence of COVID-19, with its devastating effect on Black people and other people of color, and protests spurred by Floyd's death have raised awareness of systemic racism and remarkable momentum to uproot it. Realities long understood and endured in Black communities have now been inescapably revealed to the rest of the country. For those interested in peacebuilding, conflict resolution, and racial justice, the post-COVID context presents an opportunity and a challenge. Conflict resolution can engage more with activists and social movements, think more deeply about how systems change takes place, and become more explicit about political values, positionality, and vision for a world without systemic racism. Urban communities are the ideal places to develop and sustain hybrid governance comprised of grassroots activists and those working within existing institutions. Our field is in the midst of a shift toward conflict resolution that engages more actively with conflict escalation and an approach to peacebuilding that is systemic in not only its analysis but its practices.

Notes

1 Clyde W. Yancy, "COVID-19 and African Americans," *JAMA* 323, no. 19 (2020): 1891–92, https://doi.org/10.1001/jama.2020.6548.
2 Wei-jie Guan, Wen-hua Liang, Yi Zhao, Heng-rui Liang, Zi-sheng Chen, Yi-min Li, Xiao-qing Liu et al, "Comorbidity and Its Impact on 1590 Patients with COVID-19 in China: A Nationwide Analysis," *The European Respiratory Journal* 55, no. 5 (2020), doi:10.1183/13993003.00547-2020.
3 E. Gould and H. Shierholz, "Not Everybody Can Work from Home: Black and Hispanic Workers Are Much Less Likely to Be Able to Telework," *Economic Policy Institute*, 2020, accessed April 16, 2020, https://Www. Epi. Org/Blog/Black-and-Hispanic-Workers-Are-Much-Less-Likely-to-Be-Able-To work-from-Home/.
4 Stephen Chilton and Maria Stalzer Wyant Cuzzo, "Habermas's Theory of Communicative Action as a Theoretical Framework for Mediation Practice," *Conflict Resolution Quarterly* 22, no. 3 (2005): 325–48.
5 Angela Y. Davis, *Freedom Is a Constant Struggle: Ferguson, Palestine, and the Foundations of a Escobar, Arturo. Territories of Difference: Place, Movements, Life, Redes* (Durham: Duke University Press, 2008); Angela Y. Davis, *Movement* (Chicago: Haymarket Books, 2016); Mona Lilja, Mikael Baaz, Michael Schulz, and Stellan Vinthagen, "How Resistance Encourages Resistance:

Theorizing the Nexus Between Power, 'Organised Resistance' and 'Everyday Resistance'," *Journal of Political Power* 10, no. 1 (2017): 40–54.

6 Mara Schoeny and Wallace Warfield, "Reconnecting Systems Maintenance with Social Justice: A Critical Role for Conflict Resolution," *Negotiation Journal* 16, no. 3 (2000): 253–68, doi:10.1111/j.1571-9979.2000.tb00217.x.

7 Patricia Hill Collins and Sirma Bilge, *Intersectionality* (Chicester: John Wiley & Sons, 2020); Kimberlé W. Crenshaw, *On Intersectionality: Essential Writings* (New York: The New Press, 2017).

8 Graeme Chesters, "Global Complexity and Global Civil Society," *Voluntas: International Journal of Voluntary and Nonprofit Organizations* 15, no. 4 (2004): 323–42.

9 Alexis Pauline Gumbs, "Prophecy in the Present Tense: Harriet Tubman, the Combahee Pilgrimage, and Dreams Coming True," *Meridians* 12, no. 2 (2014): 142–52, doi:10.2979/meridians.12.2.142; Patricia S. Parker, *Ella Baker's Catalytic Leadership: A Primer on Community Engagement and Communication for Social Justice* (Berkeley: University of California Press, 2020).

10 Kristian Davis Bailey, "Black – Palestinian Solidarity in the Ferguson – Gaza Era," *American Quarterly* 67, no. 4 (2015): 1017–26.

11 Sarah J. Jackson and Brooke Foucault Welles, "# Ferguson Is Everywhere: Initiators in Emerging Counterpublic Networks," *Information, Communication & Society* 19, no. 3 (2016): 397–418.

12 K. E. Boulding, *Three Faces of Power* (Newbury Park: Sage, 1990).

13 Lederach, *The Moral Imagination*.

14 Destin Jenkins, "What Does It Really Mean to Invest In Black Communities?," June 29, 2020, www.thenation.com/article/society/invest-divest-police/.

15 Shawn Ginwright, "Building a Pipeline for Justice: Understanding Youth Organizing and the Leadership Pipeline," Occasional Paper 10, Occasional Paper Series on Youth Organizing. Funders' 2010 Collaborative on Youth Organizing, http://fcyo.org/resources/ops-10-building-a-pipeline-for-justice-understanding-youth-organizing-and-the-leadership-pipeline.

16 Arthur Romano and David Ragland, "Truth-Telling from the Margins: Exploring Black-Led Responses to Police Violence and Systemic Humiliation," in *Systemic Humiliation in America: Finding Dignity within Systems of Degradation*, ed. Daniel Rothbart, 145–72 (Cham: Springer International Publishing, 2018), doi:10.1007/978-3-319-70679-5_7.

17 Adrienne Brown, "Suspensions and Referrals to Law Enforcement of African American Students Pre and Post Restorative Justice," *Electronic Theses and Dissertations*, 2019, https://stars.library.ucf.edu/etd/6312; Fania E. Davis, Mikhail Lyubansky, and Mara Schiff, "Restoring Racial Justice," *Emerging Trends in the Social and Behavioral Sciences* (2015): 1–16, https://doi.org/10.1002/9781118900772.etrds0288; Thalia González, "Addressing Racial Disparities in Discipline through Restorative Justice," in *Closing the School Discipline Gap: Equitable Remedies for Excessive Exclusion*, ed. Daniel J. Losen (New York: Teachers College Press, 2015), 22.

18 Rachel Herzing, "Big Dreams and Bold Steps Toward a Police-Free Future," *Truthout*, 2015.

19 Christopher Gray, "Brandon Anderson's RAHEEM Has Leveraged Technology and Data to Help Thousands of Black People Report Police Misconduct," *Forbes*, June 10, 2020, www.forbes.com/sites/christophergray/2020/06/10/

brandon-andersons-raheem-has-leveraged-technology-and-data-to-help-thousands-of-black-people-report-police-misconduct/.

20 Solomon Gustavo, "What We Know (and Don't Know) so Far about the Effort to Dismantle the Minneapolis Police Department," *MinnPost*, July 9, 2020, www.minnpost.com/metro/2020/07/what-we-know-and-dont-know-so-far-about-the-effort-to-dismantle-the-minneapolis-police-department/.

21 Arthur Romano,"Police Should Put Away the Military Gear and Build Connections with Young People," *The Conversation*, 2014, accessed July 14, 2020, http://theconversation.com/police-should-put-away-the-military-gear-and-build-connections-with-young-people-44947.

10 The gendered frontlines

Perpetuated inequalities or a reimagined future

Sheherazade Jafari

Historical research suggests that periods of social crisis and postcrisis recovery can have profound effects on gender relationships in diverse communities and workplaces, as well as in relation to family roles and structures. The current crisis is already known to have placed women working outside the home in a particularly vulnerable position, and analysts are beginning to assess its impact on gender relations in communities of unmarried people as well as in the family. This essay describes the longer-term effects relevant to gender relations and conflict and discusses the implications of these trends for conflict resolution.

In China's Henan province, a mother and her two children wandered the streets after her husband beat her and kicked them out of the house. Since they were hungry and with no access to food or transportation during the country's COVID-19 lockdown, a distant relative finally managed to convince police officers to help the mother and children leave their city toward safety (Wanging 2020).[1]

In the United States, Keshia Williams describes how staff at the nursing home where she works (the great majority of whom are women) balanced their long hours and sudden lack of childcare when schools shut down: one helped to watch the child of another who worked the night shift, who then watched the other mother's child during the day shift. A shortage of supplies meant that Keshia received one N95 mask a week, even though she spent each morning screening residents for the virus (Robertson and Gebeloff 2020).[2]

When her labor started at 5 am, Neelam Kumari Gautam and her husband traveled to eight different hospitals across New Delhi but were turned away at each one because of overcrowding or because doctors were afraid the couple might be infected. She began to have trouble breathing, but still could not get help. Neelam died just after 8 pm, as did her unborn son (Gettleman and Raj 2020).[3]

Gender analysts have long argued that paying attention to the gendered impacts of crises brings critical insight on how to best respond, while not doing so further exacerbates inequities. The global COVID-19 pandemic is no exception. Existing gender inequalities play a profound role on how different people are impacted in specific ways during the crisis, as well as their chances for survival or ability to "bounce back" in a post-corona world. Indeed, gender equality itself is an important predictor of a country's security, stability, and resilience. This chapter brings an intersectional gender lens to examine the effects of the COVID-19 crisis and to consider what this forecasts for the future. What we see is that the frontlines of the pandemic are highly gendered, and unless our response takes this seriously, the post-corona world will be one of particularly heightened gender inequities, and therefore, greater instability and conflict for many.

Despite overwhelming evidence that inequalities get worse during crisis situations, and that already marginalized groups are disproportionately impacted, a gender lens continues to be left out of the analysis and design of responses. Gender analysis entails asking how socially constructed roles and identities impact people's experiences and opportunities, with a particular focus on how gender intersects with other social identities such as race, class, ethnicity, age, sexuality, and disability (Smith 2020).[4] Applying an intersectional gender lens helps to make visible the social conditions and power relations – including norms, divisions of labor, and access to resources – that give rise to inequalities, and is therefore fundamental to understanding the impacts of conflicts and crises and how proposed interventions might help or ultimately exacerbate the situation.

A gendered crisis

Current data show that slightly more men than women are being infected with and dying from the virus worldwide (Haneef and Kalyanpur 2020, 2).[5] Yet women are disproportionately carrying the weight of the impact – especially if they are women of color, poor, or part of an at-risk community. Globally, women make up 70% of the health and social sector workforce (Ibid, 4) and 85% of nurses in hospitals (Mlambo-Ngcuka and Ramos 2020). Yet, they earn 28% less than men (Haneef and Kalyanpur 2020, 5). Of U.S. healthcare workers who have become infected, 73% are women (Robertson and Gebeloff 2020). The food provision sector also continued after economies shutdown, and in the United States women make up two-thirds of grocery store and fast food workers (Robertson and Gebeloff 2020). Women of color are more likely to be doing these essential, frontline jobs – whether in health care, elderly or child care, or food and other service industries – than anyone else (Schnall 2020).[6]

The pandemic's toll on the economy also has a disproportionate impact on women. In the United States, more than one-third of women experienced a significant disruption to their income, including through being furloughed, laid off, or receiving a pay cut or reduction of hours. Black women experienced these setbacks twice as much as white men (Miliband and Sandberg 2020). Globally, the far majority of the informal sector is made up of women, who often work for low wages, in unsafe conditions, and without the protection of labor laws. When Bangladesh closed its garment manufacturing sector due to canceled orders from mainly Western-based companies, its workforce – 85% of whom are women (Mlambo-Ngcuka and Ramos) – were forced to return to overcrowded slums and villages, with no savings or even access to basic sanitation (Suhrawardi 2020).[7]

Further, as schools and childcare facilities closed in many places, the impact has been largely felt by women, who perform about 76% of the total hours of unpaid care work, nearly three times as much as men (Haneef and Kalyanpur 2020, 8). For single mothers (80% of single-parent households in the United States are women), the double burden is magnified (Time's Up Foundation 2020). Further, while governments have urged people to stay home to stop the spread of the virus, for victims of domestic violence home is not a safe option. Spain saw a 47% increase to its national domestic violence hotline, whereas the UN-supported hotlines in Ukraine saw a 113% increase (Heath and Rayasam 2020).[8] We know this is likely a fraction of total cases, however, as generally less than 40% of women seek help or report a crime (Mlambo-Ngcuka and Ramos 2020). In China, one nonprofit found that 90% of the causes of reported domestic violence were pandemic related (Wanging, 2020).

As health systems become overwhelmed, resources and personnel are being diverted from other care, including maternal health. Unfortunately, we already know that maternal health risks rise during crises; during the Ebola outbreak in West Africa, the maternal mortality rate (already one of the highest in the world) increased by 75% as maternal health clinics closed in affected areas and other clinics diverted resources or refused care until after Ebola results were obtained, often when it was too late for the woman needing urgent care (Smith 2019, 362). The tragic story of Neelam at the start of this chapter suggests a similar situation with the COVID pandemic. Fragile, conflict- or crisis-affected states are particularly vulnerable, where the majority of maternal deaths occur (Haneef and Kalyanpur 2020, 5). Yet the United States also has one of the worst rates among developed countries, with Black women three to four times more likely to have a pregnancy-related death than white women, a statistic that has not changed in over six decades (Maternal Health Task Force 2020).

Suggestions to socially distance, wash hands frequently, and wear a mask are unrealistic for many poorer communities, but perhaps nowhere more than among refugee and migrant populations. Already overcrowded camps with weak water and sanitation systems are now facing dire conditions (Haneef and Kalyanpur 2020, 3). Women refugees and migrants are particularly vulnerable, often forced to travel long distances for water and food for their families, and who experience high rates of gender-based violence (GBV) even without the pressure of a global pandemic. Bosnia's Vucjuk camp deliberately cut off water supplies to force inhabitants to relocate, France's lockdowns prevented adequate deliveries of food and water to the Calais settlements, and in many other places, thousands are being turned away at the borders under the guise of preventing the spread of infection. Iain Byrne, Head of Amnesty's Refugees and Migrants Rights team, notes that "in many camps death by starvation is now reported to be a bigger threat than the virus itself" (Amnesty International 2020).[9]

Much of the same, or worse

The corona crisis is undoubtedly a gendered crisis. If our approach remains as is – without adequate attention to the gendered impacts and without deliberate interventions and resource allocation based on an intersectional gender analysis – we can expect that circumstances for women and other vulnerable communities will grow increasingly worse. Sadly, it does not take a stretch of the imagination to consider where we might be in 5–10 years, as we have enough examples from past conflict and crises situations to know what to expect. In fact, we are already seeing the signs.

The economic downturn triggered by the pandemic will have a widespread impact, but its impact on women will likely be long-term and difficult to recover. During the 2008 financial crisis, women lost significantly more jobs than men, and gained just 36% of the jobs that were recovered (Time's Up Foundation 2020). Women are in lower paying jobs on average, and make up the majority of the informal sector with no job security, making it particularly difficult to have savings. The COVID pandemic will likely increase poverty levels as it reaches more vulnerable populations, which directly impacts child marriage rates; a reduction of 10% GPA per capital will result in an estimated 5.6 million more child marriages within the next ten years (UNFPA 2020).[10] The burden of unpaid care work will also continue, taking a toll on women's physical and psychological health and increasing their exposure to the virus.

If other conflict and crisis situations are any indication, there is a huge risk that GBV rates will continue to rise as stress levels and economic hardship increase. In fact, intimate partner violence may be the most prevalent form of violence to women during emergencies (CARE 2020). UNFPA estimates that for every three months of COVID lockdown, we can expect an additional 15 million cases of GBV globally (UNFPA 2020). Yet support services –already limited and struggling for funds in many places – will be further weakened as resources are diverted to containing the outbreak, and as people fear being infected at the remaining overcrowded shelters.

Finally, refugee and displaced women are acutely vulnerable as travel is limited, humanitarian services such as the provision of sanitary supplies are interrupted, and GBV rates increase with little to no options for support (CARE 2020). According to Amnesty International, refugee and migrant camps will be the "epicenter of the pandemic" unless urgent action is taken (2020).

An opportunity for transformative change

As the COVID crisis magnifies the harmful defects in our economic and social systems, the current moment presents an opportunity to not just stop the spread of the virus and bring back the economy for the benefit of some, but to challenge the inequitable structures that continue to perpetuate injustice and instability for so many. What would need to happen for a truly just and equitable world to exist? How can we apply the lessons learned from decades of research on and experience in conflicts and crises, which consistently point to the need to take an intersectional gender approach – and which demonstrate that the COVID crisis is a gendered crisis? How might conflict resolution researchers and practitioners help to reimagine and rebuild a new reality? Indeed, peacebuilders are often called to consider how to transcend the worst cycles of violence and to imagine the possibility of change (Lederach 2005).

Put simply, such a future could be possible if we make supporting and protecting women, girls, and other at-risk and vulnerable populations a priority. For conflict resolvers and crisis mitigators, this requires centering the voices of women and other vulnerable groups in all our efforts. As the ones most impacted, women are in a prime position to identify the trends within their communities and must be involved in all aspects of the design of responses – including the allocation of resources. Women's formal and informal community groups and networks have been working as first responders and carry critical knowledge on the situation, and play an important role in reimagining a better future for their communities. Women also need to be involved at all levels of leadership – from community decision-making bodies to national and international agencies. As it is, the UN's $2 billion humanitarian appeal to stop COVID-19's spread to vulnerable communities hardly mentioned women and girls (Miliband and Sandberg 2020). Although women make up the majority of health and social care workers, few hold decision-making positions (Haneef and Kalyanpur 2020, 4). Indeed, the United States' original Coronavirus Task Force included zero women.

Yet women often bring different qualities of leadership, which appear to be particularly needed in this crisis. A series of articles circulated a few months into the pandemic featured leaders whose countries are doing better than most at managing the crisis. What do they all have in common, the articles asked? All are women. Among them, New Zealand's Jacinda Arden was called "one of the most effective leaders on the planet" for her swift, effective, yet sympathetic handling of the crisis (Friedman 2020). Taiwan's president Tsai Ing-wen was similarly praised for her quick response and open communication. Putting aside their shared gender, the praise of their leadership has focused on their willingness to talk with and collaborate across health, social, and other sectors; their empathy in the face of deep tragedy among their people; their flexibility and their decisiveness; and their ability to bring a "whole life perspective" that acknowledges people's various needs and struggles at work and at home (Schnall 2020). Their examples of leadership stand in stark contrast to, for example, U.S. President Donald Trump, Brazilian President Jair Bolsonaro, and Indian Prime Minister Narendra Modi, who rejected guidance from the scientific community and sought to "win" the war against the virus with their own might. What the COVID pandemic is revealing, however, is that such forms of "super masculine" leadership (or what is called toxic masculinity) leads to chaos and ultimately defeat, and the way to truly "win" against the pandemic is to collaborate, acknowledge people's lived experiences with the crisis, and indeed, demonstrate a sense of empathy. While women are often conditioned to take on such roles, these traits need not be gender specific, but provide critical insight for conflict resolvers on what is needed for an effective and transformative response to the crisis.

The COVID pandemic and other crises also show that structural supports such as access to safe schools and health facilities, health insurance, affordable child care, and paid sick and family leave are far from luxuries but essential for building resilient and successful economies and equitable communities. Services that particularly support women and vulnerable communities, such as domestic violence shelters and maternal health facilities, must also be acknowledged as essential, with adequate resources and personal protective equipment for their frontline workers.

A few months into the pandemic, the situation is challenging and the future – if we follow the current trajectory – looks dire. But the crisis provides us with a critical opportunity to shift course and repair the broken systems that leave so many women and other at-risk groups vulnerable to inequalities, and their communities to ongoing crises and conflicts. By applying an intersectional gender lens to their work, conflict resolution researchers and practitioners can help us reimagine and build a future that is equitable for all.

Notes

1 Zhang Wanging, "Domestic Violence Cases Surge During COVID-19 Epidemic," *Sixth Tone*, March 2, 2020, www.sixthtone.com/news/1005253/domestic-violence-cases-surge-during-covid-19-epidemic.
2 Campbell Robertson and Robert Gebeloff, "How Millions of Women Became the Most Essential Workers in America," *New York Times*, April 18, 2020, www.nytimes.com/2020/04/18/us/coronavirus-women-essential-workers.html.
3 Jeffrey Gettleman and Suhasini Raj, "8 Hospitals in 15 Hours: A Pregnant Woman's Crisis in the Pandemic," *New York Times*, June 21, 2020, www.nytimes.com/2020/06/21/world/asia/coronavirus-india-hospitals-pregnant.html.
4 Julie Smith, "Overcoming the 'Tyranny of the Urgent': Integrating Gender into Disease Outbreak Preparedness and Response," *Gender & Development* 27 (2019): 355–69.
5 Christina Haneef and Anushka Kalyanpur, "Global Rapid Gender Analysis for COVID-19," *CARE and International Rescue Committee*, 2020, www.rescue.org/sites/default/files/document/4676/globalrgacovidrdm33120final.pdf.
6 Marianne Schnall, " 'These Extraordinary Times Call for Extraordinary Giving': 12 Leaders in Women's Philanthropy Speak Out," *Forbes*, June 23, 2020, www.forbes.com/sites/marianneschnall/2020/06/23/12-leaders-in-womens-philanthropy-speak-out/#59f29e235a70; Marianne Schnall, "Ten Prominent Women Spotlight the Need for Women's Leadership During the Pandemic and Beyond," *Forbes*, May 18, 2020.
7 Rebecca Suhrawardi, "Collapse of Bangladesh's Garment Industry During Coronavirus Leaves Its Workers More Vulnerable Than Ever," *Forbes*, March 30, 2020, www.forbes.com/sites/rebeccasuhrawardi/2020/03/30/collapse-of-banglade shs-garment-industry-leaves-its-workers-more-vulnerable-than-ever-during-coronavirus/#1e453d74f27e.
8 Ryan Heath and Renuka Rayasam, "Covid's War on Women," *Politico.com*, April 29, 2020, www.politico.com/newsletters/politico-nightly-coronavirus-spe cial-edition/2020/04/29/covids-war-on-women-489076; www.forbes.com/sites/marianneschnall/2020/05/18/ten-prominent-women-spotlight-need-forwomens-leadershipduring-pandemic/#30d4c6712498.
9 Amnesty International, "Ignored by COVID-19 Responses, Refugees Face Starvation," May 13, 2020, www.amnesty.org/en/latest/news/2020/05/refugees-and-migrants-being-forgotten-in-covid19-crisis-response/.
10 UNFPA, "Impact of the COVID-19 Pandemic on Family Planning and Ending Gender-Based Violence, Female Genital Mutilation and Child Marriage," April 27, 2020, www.unfpa.org/resources/impact-covid-19-pandemic-family-planning-and-ending-gender-based-violence-female-genital.

References

All web-based sources accessed on July 15, 2020.

Cockburn, Cynthia. "The Continuum of Violence: A Gender Perspective on War and Peace." In *Sites of Violence: Gender and Conflict Zones*, edited by Wenona Giles and Jennifer Hyndman. Berkeley: University of California Press, 2004.

Long, Heather. "The Big Factor Holding Back the U.S. Economic Recovery: Child Care." *Washington Post*, July 3, 2020. www.washingtonpost.com/business/2020/07/03/big-factor-holding-back-us-economic-recovery-child-care/.

Tickner, J. Ann. *Gendering World Politics: Issues and Approaches in the Post-Cold War Era*. New York: Columbia University Press, 2001.

Ventura Alfaro, María José. "Feminist Solidarity Networks Have Multiplied Since the COVID-19 Outbreak in Mexico." *Interface: A Journal for and About Social Movements* (May 2020). www.interfacejournal.net/wp-content/uploads/2020/05/Ventura-Alfaro-1.pdf.

11 Internal and eternal insecurity

Impact of crisis on religious group identity

Charles Davidson

The impact of global crises on the social psychology and spiritual development of those forced to tolerate a high degree of fear and uncertainty is not well understood. This chapter describes the effects of these conditions on people's feelings of competency and agency and on their moral or religious feelings and demands. It explores the implications of a period of unexpected change for religious and values-based organizations. It concludes by analyzing the growing threat of intensified cultural conflict and the prospects of fostering mass education in "compassionate reasoning" as a basis for more sustainable conflict resolution.

Introduction

During the current COVID-19 crisis, a subset of American White Evangelical Protestants (WEPs) continue to gather in close quarters, travel on public conveyances, and refuse to wear medical masks as a symbol of their collective religious identity, declaring, "God will protect us." Some consider expert-advised pandemic responses an attack on conservative politicians and agendas (Stewart 2020),[1] not recognizing that rejecting expert advice creates a unique and dangerous health risk for many. This contention is yet another iteration in a long-entrenched battle between traditional Protestant Evangelicalism and several of its perceived foes, including modernism, progressivism, and liberalism. This has further exacerbated inter-protestant conflict and conflict between WEPs and outsiders and will likely persist well after the current pandemic subsides. This chapter examines the roots of this conflict and its possible long-lasting consequences for American society. It concludes that conflict resolution among religious groups during eras of crisis should include the understanding that many believers fear the loss of their eternal destiny and group identity more than they fear sickness or death.

Conflict among white Evangelical protestants

According to the Pew Research Center (2011),[2] Evangelicals are "saved" by being "born again," believe the bible to be God's word delivered to humanity, and often share their faith with others. Descended from the "pietical" Christians of the past who made evangelism a necessary requisite of faith, Evangelicals do not constitute a clearly defined group, but rather evince traits found among many Protestant groups (Ware 2011,[3] 35 and Pew 2011). While Evangelicals make up some 25% of the American population and are therefore quite diverse (Masci, D and Smith, G. 2018),[4] WEPs mentioned in this work tend to espouse socially and fiscally conservative sentiments and are both pro-capitalist and anti-welfare (Deckman, M., Cox, D., Jones, R., & Cooper, B. 2017).[5]

In general, WEPs argue for a more "values-based" system of culture and government and decry the vices allegedly promoted by liberal politics in the American sociopolitical milieu, though they often rally behind politicians who embrace these vices in pursuit of political and economic power (Howe 2019).[6] WEP collective identity markers also include a suspicion of science and "the experts," sexual beliefs supporting abstinence, traditional gender norms and heterosexuality, denial of manmade climate change, devotion to capitalism and economic growth as a political priority, and, importantly, the public display of support for such ideas. Indeed, the very idea that one is Evangelical demands that one's beliefs be publicly promoted and "evangelized," even if those ideas are often largely political.

Why do such strong oppositional sentiments exist among American evangelicals, especially when many of these sentiments seem to counter basic benefits to society at large? First, twice as many evangelicals as non-evangelicals have long asserted that science and religion are in conflict. As noted by Katherine Stewart (2020), "at least since the 19th century, when the proslavery theologian Robert Lewis Dabney attacked the physical sciences as 'theories of unbelief,' hostility to science has characterized the more extreme forms of religious nationalism in the United States." A large portion of Evangelicals regard science as something conducted by faithless outsiders and are therefore suspicious of scientific motives, products, and those who influence the scientific community (Brown 2015).[7] Second, evangelicals on the whole perceive themselves as being under attack by the scientific community. Not only do they suspect the motives of scientists but also almost 60% feel that they are deliberately targeted by these experts (Brown 2015). Third, many WEPs view science as a tool used by the left to oppose conservative and capitalist models in an attempt to seize cultural and political control (Stewart 2020).

This WEP-Progressive "culture war" has been expressed both actively and passively during the current pandemic. For instance, Christian leaders and pastors such as Guillermo Maldonado and Rodney Howard-Browne encouraged churchgoers to continue to meet together, citing faith as a reason to gather in spite of the risk; Howard-Browne even mocked those who feared the pandemic as "pansies" (Stewart, 2020). Some pastors such as Steve Hotze and Tony Spell decried the pandemic as either "fake news" (Hotze) or as politically motivated (Spell) (Stewart 2020). Others were more passive, declaring that God would protect them, in spite of the fact that many (including acquaintances of this writer) have paid for this decision with their lives. During the summer of 2020, large churches in western and southern states of the United States, some with participants numbering in the thousands, continued to meet despite the second explosion of COVID-19 cases (Cabeza 2020).[8]

The roots of this conflict are found in an extended struggle that traditionalist Christians have waged since the late nineteenth century against modernism and liberalism. While it is candidly argued that Evangelicalism is always at war with whatever is "current" in the United States (Wallace 2005),[9] conflicts with modernism have continued since 1891, at least. According to Pultz (1996),[10] the conflict was sparked by the Charles A. Briggs heresy trial – a proceeding brought by religious conservatives against a well-known Presbyterian theologian, who, in a speech at Union Theological Seminary in 1891, "attacked 'Traditionalism,' later known as Fundamentalism, and espoused an interpretation of the Bible in the light of the 'Higher Criticism.' The Higher Criticism was a method of investigating facts based on scientific investigation, inductive research, and a relative system of values."

Modernism opened the doors that enabled science, intellectualism, and reason to begin to challenge long-held beliefs and systems within American Protestantism (Bebbington (1990) and Hunter (1992)[11]). The tendency to question certain fundamental ideas upon which Protestant faith had been built, including using the Bible as the sole source of inspiration of one's faith, established a barrier between modernists and traditionalists. The more famous Scopes "Monkey" Trial brought the theory of evolution to the cultural fore, and the inter-protestant conflict between modernists and traditionalists, now a source of widespread discussion and controversy, became entrenched. As J.D. Hunter (1992) asserts in his seminal work, *Culture Wars*, religious conflict in America is no longer primarily defined as inter-religious, but rather as conflict between "orthodox" and "progressive" members of the same groups. Hunter states, "what seems to be a myriad of self-contained cultural disputes actually amounts to a fairly comprehensive and momentous struggle to define the meaning of America"

The social-structural basis for Evangelical-Modernist conflict is still not as well understood as one might hope. Hofstadter (1960 and 1966)[12] argued earlier that the rise of progressive religion was related to the socio-economic changes that produced a new educated, urbanized middle class and that alienated rural residents and others marginalized by the late industrial economy. Though some may argue along these lines that the theological liberals accepted and integrated modernist thought in Evangelicalism, Pultz (1996) maintains that liberals within the Evangelical movement did not necessarily embrace substantive modernist positions, but, rather, encouraged openness, inclusivity, and tolerance. When these procedural norms were rejected by fundamentalists, conflict ensued, leading some to declare that liberal theology was "a different religion" entirely (Pultz 1996).

WEP pandemic collective identity, boundary maintenance, and costly signaling

WEPs should not be judged as uniquely misanthropic in their approach to collective identity. Many rely on a collective faith identity to elevate feelings of confidence and belonging which requires boundary maintenance in overt ways (Irons 2001).[13] Across faith traditions, "costly signaling" demonstrates outward investment that may be maladaptive or detrimental to the individual but that demonstrates devoutness to the group (Tuzin 1982).[14] During times of heightened fear, the faithful from many traditions project their group identity to solidify perceived membership and winnow weaker members for the sake of group sustainability and integrity (Irons 2001). Within religion, such signals may include snake handling, fasting, sacrifice or donation of resources, self-harm, cutting, or mutilation of several types, and many other acts. While these acts can be harmful to the individual, they address the "free rider" problem by exposing the undevout outsider and helping to maintain group integrity (Irons 2001)

Anthropologist Mary Douglas' work on religious purity, danger, dirt, and pollution forms a foundation of contemporary thought on this type of boundary maintenance. "Dirt," or social deviance within a religious collective identity, "offends against order." Rarely, however, is social deviance defined by the existence of a particular individual within the WEP collective identity; rather, it is the associated social system that must be expunged, which aligns with Douglas' aphorism, "where there is dirt there is system" (Douglas 1966, 36).[15] Christian Smith (1998, 92)[16] adds to our understanding of boundary maintenance by noting that "identity distinctions are always created through the use of socially constructed symbolic markers that establish group boundaries. It is through languages, rituals, artifacts, creeds, practices, narratives – in short, the stuff of human cultural production – that social groups construct their sense of self and difference from others."

During this time of worldwide health concern, WEP collective identity boundaries are complicated by the necessity for some to reject widely embraced preventative health measures because they are either prescribed by those who occupy a different and "opposing" collective identity space, or because the views presented run counter to those deemed the proper authority. As Dr. Anthony Fauci commented on June 17, 2020,

> *One of the problems we face in the United States is that unfortunately, there is a combination of an anti-science bias that people are – for reasons that sometimes are, you know, inconceivable and not understandable – they just don't believe science and they don't believe authority.*

This collective identity boundary exacerbates the risk of sickness to the individual, threatens the lives of others, and is arguably one of the first times that Evangelical costly signaling has become dangerous for "outsiders" writ large. For instance, some Evangelicals I have spoken with said that they felt pressured by their peers to commune in close proximity without respiratory protection and did so out of a fear of offense or being perceived as lacking in their shared faith.

Long-term consequences and implications

Identity signaling during times of crisis has practical implications for conflict resolution in the mid- and post-pandemic world. Should any solution be reached that would encourage WEPs to embrace health precautions, it will very likely originate from a member of their own group or a trusted authority. Messages from deviant "outsiders" are likely to be ignored. This situation illustrates a reality that has more far-reaching implications as well. Oftentimes, during any crisis, health-related or otherwise, the fear for one's safety, and especially the safety of others is not of primary importance, nor is it the primary source of fear for the faithful. Instead, it is the prospect of the loss of collective identity membership (especially among religious groups) that is the most troubling to some. Conflict resolution must therefore first recognize that to the Evangelical, dismissal from the group means a loss of identity, community, and eternity.

What consequences does this conflict therefore hold for the future, especially during the lengthy period of recovery of these multiple crises? First, given the current political climate paired with the costly signaling that has now crossed over into being "costly" for others, it is unlikely that these signals will simply retract. Instead, as has occurred throughout American history, divisions between progressive and traditionalist Protestants exacerbated by the pandemic response are unlikely to mend. Second, politicians supported by districts comprised of large WEP voting blocs are likely to continue to endorse positions friendly to Evangelical groups even if they seemingly harm the population as a whole. Third, the long-term ramifications of this conflict may well diminish America's ability to influence and participate in the world society. Not only WEPs but many Americans who have refused to wear masks and insist on continuing life as usual for a variety of other identity-based or political reasons have caused a dramatic spike in new COVID-19 cases, prompting other states to close their borders to Americans.

Opportunities for resolution and paths forward

The challenge of communicating this harm is that outsider-delivered messages of caution appear as attacks on group identity. Communication must therefore respect identity boundaries and equip voices to communicate the need for preventative and reactive measures. These responses must also be developed with an understanding of the polarization of modern communication. This can be done in four ways:

First, messages of compassionate reasoning can be facilitated by those in the "middle." Moderate members of the Evangelical and modernist communities possess the capacity to understand the need for change without appearing to be yielding to outside pressures. One of the main challenges to this solution will come from competing messages of polarization in today's media. As Patterson (1992)[17] remarked "By catering to popular tastes and to a market that thrives on superficial and sensational rhetoric, communication technologies foster greater polarization, highlighting extreme voices while muffling those in the middle." How much more so is this true today than in 1992? Relatedly, messengers should be equipped with conflict resolution language that is constructed with respect to group principles and virtues.

Second, leadership such as that provided by pastors, local business leaders, or public figures (authors, public speakers, evangelists) may substitute, in WEP eyes, for that offered by politicians, academics, and public health officials. Of this group, messengers could normalize pandemic responses by actively demonstrating preventative measures both inside and outside of group spaces.

Third, WEPs should be engaged with cross-faith groups that share similar sociopolitical goals. It is understood from both research (such as Hunter 1992) and from personal experience that conservative WEPs have more in common with orthodox members of other faiths than they often do with progressive members of their own, often without realizing it. Therefore, it would be advantageous to formulate a dialogue between these groups to develop paths of strategy forward so that the element of isolation is diminished. In this way, feelings of the need for delineation from the rest of American society may also decrease. Importantly, this dialogue should include conservative but *nominal* Evangelicals as well. As J.D. Vance's *Hillbilly Elegy* (2016)[18] shows, while Jesus may be the nominal Evangelical's "God," collective identity for some may be much less about the application of faith in everyday life, and more about the sustainability of culture based upon protestant traditions.

Finally, the possibility of intensified conflict shows the need for further study about the underlying causes of the Evangelical culture war. Though works such as Hofstadter (1960 and 1966) Hunter (1992), Ware (2011), Luhrmann (2012),[19] Vance (2016), and Howe (2019) provide much-needed insights into the development of and paths toward understanding this culture war, much has yet to be resolved as to what drives the evangelical sentiments that can so often appear to be misanthropic, and yet are based on a religion that is founded in love and care for others.

Notes

1 Katherine Stewart, "The Religious Right's Hostility to Science Is Crippling Our Coronavirus Response," *The New York Times*, March 27, 2020, www.nytimes.com/2020/03/27/opinion/coronavirus-trump-evangelicals.html.

2 Pew Research Center, "Global Christianity: A Report on the Size and Distribution of the World's Christian Population," *The Pew Forum on Religion and Public Life*, December 2011, www.pewforum.org/files/2011/12/Christianity-fullreport-web.pdf.

3 Alan Ware, *Political Conflict in America* (New York: Palgrave Macmillan, 2011).

4 D. Masci and G. Smith, "5 Facts About U.S. Evangelical Protestants," *Pew Research Center, Fact Tank*, March 1, 2018, accessed July 10, 2020, www.pewresearch.org/fact-tank/2018/03/01/5-facts-about-u-s-evangelical-protestants/.

5 Melissa Deckman, Dan Cox, Robert Jones, and Betsy Cooper, "Faith and the Free Market: Evangelicals, the Tea Party, and Economic Attitudes," *Politics and Religion* 10, no. 1 (2017): 82–110; T. W. Cooper, "Emerging, Emergent, Emergence: Boundary Maintenance, Definition Construction, and Legitimation Strategies in the Establishment of a Post-Evangelical Subculture," *Journal for the Scientific Study of Religion* 56 (2017): 398–417.

6 Ben Howe, *The Immoral Majority: Why Evangelicals Chose Political Power Over Christian Values* (New York: Harper Collins, 2019).

7 Sarah Kropp Brown, "Are Evangelicals Anti-Science?" *National Association of Evangelicals*, Fall 2015, accessed June 30, 2020, www.nae.net/evangelicals-anti-science/on.

8 Garrett Cabeza, "Christ Church Service Draws 1,000 People," *Moscow-Pullman Daily News*, June 30, 2020, accessed July 2, 2020, https://dnews.com/corona

virus/christ-church-service-draws-1-000-people/article_7ecbcf3c-7ce6–5b8e-a5c3-f4bc43553e0e.html.

9 Daniel Wallace, "A Clash of Cultures: Evangelism in a Postmodern World (Part I)," *Bible.org*, accessed July 9, 2020, https://bible.org/article/clash-cultures-evangelism-postmodern-world-part-i.

10 David Pultz, "The Fundamentalist / Modernist Conflict," *The First Presbyterian Church in the City of New York*, 1996, www.fpcnyc.org/the-fundamentalist-modernist-conflict/.

11 James Davison Hunter, *Culture Wars: The Struggle to Defend America* (New York: Basic Books, 1992).

12 Richard Hofstadter, *The Age of Reform* (New York: Vintage, 1960); Richard Hofstadter, *Anti-Intellectualism in American Life* (New York: Vintage, 1966).

13 W. Irons, "Religion as a Hard-to-Fake Sign of Commitment," in *The Evolution of Commitment*, ed. Randolph Nesse, 292–309 (New York: Russell Sage Foundation, 2001).

14 D. Tuzin, "Ritual Violence Among the Ilahita Arapesh," in *Rituals of Manhood: Male Initiation in Papua New Guinea*, ed. G. H. Herdt, 321–56 (Berkeley: University of California Press, 1982).

15 Mary Douglas, *Purity and Danger* (London: Routledge and Keegan Paul, 1966).

16 Christian Smith, *American Evangelicalism: Embattled and Thriving* (Chicago: University of Chicago Press, 1998).

17 Robert W. Patterson, "Clash of Cultures," Review of *Culture Wars*, by James Davison Hunter, *Christianity Today* 36, no. 1; Proquest Central p. 60, January 13, 1992.

18 J. D. Vance, *Hillbilly Elegy: A Memoir of a Family and Culture in Crisis* (New York: HarperCollins, 2016).

19 Tanya Luhrmann, *When God Talks Back: Understanding the American Evangelical Relationship with God* (New York: Random House, 2012).

Part IV

Conflict resolution initiatives after the pandemic

12 Peace engineering in a complex pandemic world

Alpasian Özerdem and Lisa Schirch

In this essay, two leading practitioners and theorists of conflict resolution explore the relevance of "Peace Engineering" – a holistic, evidence-based approach to peacebuilding – to a society sorely in need of innovative and healing methods of resolving disputes. Given that the period of recovery following the biomedical crisis is likely to be long and stormy, a key question is how to apply sufficient resources with sufficient intelligence to open the door to "positive peace." The authors deploy practical ideas formulated by experts in community development to outline a multi-faceted approach to this complex problem.

Introduction

Peace engineering is "the application of science and engineering principles to promote and support peace," as defined by the International Federation of Educational Engineering Societies (IFEES). The primary goals of peace engineering are to prevent, mitigate, and recover from violence and to develop sustainable social and technological systems for community well-being.

An engineering project is never neutral. Whether designing a city, a building, a medicine, a machine, a social media platform, a mask or public transportation, new technologies and inventions impact relationships between people. One new engineered product or technology can alter the dynamics of a community, either creating more conflict or improving intergroup relationships. Peace engineering aims to anticipate and prevent unintended negative consequences of a new product or technology while maximizing social cohesion or positive relationships between groups.

The COVID-19 pandemic arrived in the midst of multiple other crises, as described by other chapters in this book. Humanity faces a climate crisis, and a governance crisis with growing economic inequality and a precipitous decline in support for democratic leaders and institutions. In addition, the last decade has seen a significant increase in complex humanitarian emergencies from civil war and natural disasters with record numbers of refugees and other migrants moving across borders,[1] and new awareness of the lasting impacts of colonialism, slavery, and institutionalized racism. On top of all that, or in part because of it, there are growing reports of individual depression and anxiety.[2] A post-COVID world faces interconnected threats.

The triple threat of pandemic, climate, and governance crises creates both opportunities and risks for a planet requiring rapid social change. There is a pressing need for peace engineering that addresses the interconnection between human health and well-being, the environment, and governance through assessment and planning processes that reduce risks of unintended negative impacts and improve social cohesion. While peace engineering shares some common concerns related to the subfields of environmental engineering, or engineering for social justice, peace engineering includes a more comprehensive, systematic marrying of the skills and concepts from the field of engineering with the fields of conflict resolution and peacebuilding. Peace engineering by necessity also includes commitments to environmental sustainability, social equity, entrepreneurship, transparency, community engagement, and economic development. Peaceful relationships between people require attention to the environment, the economy, and participatory governance.

Peace engineering's three interfaces

Before the COVID-19 pandemic hit the world and posed a wide range of human security challenges, peace engineering was already being considered as an emerging area of cooperation between the realms of engineering and building peace through their three primary interfaces.

The first cluster of peace engineering activities ensures that the perspectives of risk reduction and conflict sensitivity are included in every engineering and technology development project. As we have observed this throughout different eras, there is a clear interface within the nexus of technology development and peaceful societal relations. In broad terms, this type of interface would focus on how different technologies are impacting our sociopolitical and economic relations, and ultimately, contributing toward the environment of peace in that society. For example, how social media informs the way individuals relate to each other or how virtual communities of different focus and purpose are formed and mobilized in a wide range of sociopolitical settings, and ultimately their impact on peaceful relations.

In line with this risk reduction and conflict sensitivity perspective, it is also essential to ensure that engineering is undertaken in socio-economically and environmentally vulnerable environments with the principle of "do no harm," whether this is about building a housing project in Washington D.C. or a massive dam project in Turkey. As there is no neutral engineering project, the process of engineering should be undertaken with such awareness of the possibility of the exacerbation of existing conflicts or creating new ones.

The second interface also emerges from the conflict sensitivity perspective, but this time, the focus is more on how engineering or physical reconstruction could be used as a means or tool for peacebuilding in divided conflict-affected societies. Whether this is about building roads, bridges, hospitals, or irrigation systems in Afghanistan, Bosnia, or Colombia, the processes of the physical building could provide such opportunities. The methods of engineering could become as important as the result of such rebuilding and construction projects if they can address societal divisions. With that, the training of engineers with better awareness and tools of conflict resolution, for example, also becomes one of the most effective ways of rebuilding divided societies.

Finally, the third cluster of this interface could be identified as those activities focusing on the development and use of appropriate technologies for conflict prevention, humanitarian aid, and peacebuilding purposes. For example, the PeaceTech Lab of the United States Institute of Peace (USIP) works on the intersection of technology, media, Big Data to reduce violent conflict. There is also now an increasing engagement with Artificial Intelligence (AI) in the peacebuilding space, such as the processing of vast information and data in support of peace processes, which is another emerging peace engineering area of focus. A wide range of humanitarian engineering initiatives such as the development of accessible and appropriate technologies for the provision of safe water and shelter in refugee crises, or early warning systems for humanitarian crises, for example, could also be included in this group of peace engineering focus.

We would argue that each of these peace engineering interfaces will be highly critical in the post-pandemic world, as all the predictions on the future world are particularly bleak with many socio-economic and political challenges. Moreover, we are in the view that to prevent conflicts and to build peace will be much more difficult in the post-pandemic world. To address these challenges and create more just and peaceful societies, engineering and the development of appropriate technology can provide humanity with new horizons and opportunities for peace.

Peace engineering opportunities in a pandemic, climate, and governance crisis

COVID-19 created massive and immediate lifestyle changes, some positive and many negative, that interact with the climate crisis and the governance crisis. Each of these changes created new peace engineering opportunities.

Lockdowns and quarantines required millions of people to work from home, creating a boom in online meeting platforms such as Zoom or Circles. Children were not able to go to school, leading to massive increases in the time spent on technology with computer games, videos, or television. Schools struggled to find alternate ways of educating, including sending written assignments home, airing lectures on the radio or through online meeting platforms. Universities moved classes online, expanding digital technologies such as Panopto and VoiceThread for interactive online learning. While online learning and virtual meeting spaces are not new, there is a pressing need for peace engineers to make these technologies better to enable more social interaction and to reduce the negative impacts of extensive screen time.

The lockdowns also impacted mental and social well-being. Surveys indicate a spike in reports of depression and anxiety resulting from the social isolation.[3] Peace engineers could explore how technology can better address these personal crises, via free access to technology, facilitated digital mental health services and meetings like AA (Alcoholic Anonymous), matching people who are lonely with each other, or creating more public meeting spaces to enable social distancing and addressing isolation.

In the United States, protests against systemic racism, led by the Movement to Defend Black Lives, have surfaced because of a string of killings of unarmed Black men and women. These protests have taken place primarily in public. But computer engineers are creating new platforms that allow activists to meet and plan tactics online, to enable protest organizing and mass action to happen online.[4]

Carbon emissions have decreased during the COVID-19 pandemic thanks to international and domestic travel decreased as people worked from home.[5] Bicycle sales have increased as people in large cities avoided buses and subways.[6] Some cities and towns have closed off streets to enable more people to walk, bike, and eat outside. COVID-19 offers an opportunity for peace engineers to design cities that encourage walking and bicycling, and discourage driving not only in the short term, but as a test period and transition to long term urban design changes that can address the pandemic, the climate crisis, and the need for healthy exercise and social interaction to combat isolation and depression.

COVID-19 has had a range of negative impacts on the environment as well, and these too offer opportunities for peace engineers. During the lockdowns, farms were not able to harvest fruits and vegetables, which rotted in the fields. Animals raised for meat were not able to be slaughtered and processed, so they were killed and disposed of as waste. Single-use plastic masks, gloves, gowns, eating utensils, and packaging massively increased, creating greater threats to oceans, rivers, and landfills already choked with plastics. Restaurants and grocery stores had to redesign their spaces to allow social distancing.

Peace engineering could address each of these negative impacts by viewing these challenges as opportunities to improve social cohesion. How could new technologies connect farmers in new ways to communities that need food? How can new biodegradable plastics made from bamboo and corn starch replace single-use masks, gowns, and food containers? What types of sustainable materials could be used to create gloves? How can technological invention of plant-based meats take off in the midst of a pandemic that reveals again the mass cost to human and plant health of animal agriculture and mass farms? Here are some peace engineering design principles in tackling such COVID-19 world challenges.

Peace engineering design principles in a COVID-19 world

The triple bottom line for socially responsible businesses includes assessments to measure the impact of a product on "people, planet and profit."[7] Engineers can maximize their positive impact on people, planet, and profit through assessments that will reveal, anticipate, and reduce their risks of unintentional harms to people or the planet. Engineers typically design products with principles such as ease of use, improving quality of life, cost-effectiveness, and visual attractiveness. Engineers typically ask questions to identify a problem or opportunity for improving life with an engineered solution. Peace engineering introduces two additional sets of design principles: to reduce violent conflict and to maximize social cohesion or "peace."

Peace engineering design principles begin with conflict analysis to assess the "who, why, how, what, where and when" of conflict. Conflict analysis tools provide a structured research method to determine who holds a stake in the conflict, what motivates them, what forms of power they leverage with or over other stakeholders, what grievances or interests they aim to address, and when and where they plan to take action.[8]

Design principles for conflict reduction include using assessment tools to ensure the design of any new technology takes into consideration the following questions.

- Who are the stakeholders who will be affected by the problem? What is their worldview or interest in the problem?

- What in the wider context might change by addressing the current problem?
- What are the range of potential solutions to address the problem?
- What are potential second order, unintended impacts for each engineering solution to the problem?
- What can be done to minimize potential harmful impacts of an engineered solution?

Design principles for maximizing social cohesion and peace include the following:

- What are the divisions that already exist within the organization, community, or society that will be impacted by an engineered solution?
- How will an engineered solution impact those most marginalized in a society?
- How can an engineered solution help to foster social cohesion, human rights, and dignity of each member of the community?
- How can the opportunity for designing an engineered solution together with a community enable the development of a shared vision that might increase social cohesion?

Two examples illustrate how peace engineering can both reduce risks of conflict, and also intentionally include design elements that contribute to social cohesion in a complex COVID-19 world.

Engineers creating effective masks to prevent COVID-19 transmission would start with a holistic assessment. Surveys and focus groups of diverse stakeholders including health professionals, local government officials, and local populations in different regions might reveal the conflict dynamics around mask wearing. In the United States, for example, mask wearing has become highly politically charged with a president who refuses to wear a mask, and some associating mask wearing as a loss of freedom.[9] A survey might also surface design obstacles to mask wearing including physical discomfort, inability to breath, overheating, and condensation on glasses. An analysis of the context could also use big data collected by scraping Twitter, Facebook, and other social media as well as legacy media coverage of mask wearing to reveal. Engineers designing masks can combine this social analysis of mask wearing in combination with the technical requirements identified by health professionals such as types of fabric, layers, and filters that maximize health protection. Mask engineers could establish a rating system in conjunction with health experts to ensure the masks filter the maximum amount of virus particles. Mask design could also consider how to reduce further polarization or conflict. Masks with political messages such as "Make America Great Again" might be more appealing to Republicans who think mask wearing is only for Democrats. But such political messages on masks would reinforce existing political cleavages. Mask engineers that want to foster social cohesion could dream a bit bigger. Masks with messages that enforced cross-cutting identities, "Masks are for Patriots," "I wear a mask for you, you wear one for me," or "Love Your Neighbors, Wear a Mask" might inspire a more unifying social impact. Engineers might use recycled fibers or sustainably grown fabrics to reduce impact on the environment.

A second example includes the design of public handwashing centers to prevent COVID-19, particularly in regions without running water. The climate crisis has made access to water scarce, and more conflictual.[10] Engineers could begin with a stakeholder assessment to find out the locations in a community that would benefit from handwashing centers. Engineers might first apply design principles of conflict reduction by ensuring that all members of community will have equal access to water. Engineers could also apply design principles for maximizing social cohesion by intentionally forming a diverse water management committee who will work together to ensure different ethnic and religious groups, ages, and genders will each have access to water.

Conclusion

Peace engineering is an emerging area of the interface between engineering and peacebuilding. As a concept, approach, and application, it has so far primarily been developed in engineering schools.[11] However, the Jimmy and Rosalynn Carter School for Peace and Conflict Resolution of George Mason University has just initiated a peace engineering program within its Carter School Peace Labs. The program will be focusing on the earlier mentioned three interfaces of peace engineering to address the post-pandemic challenges in peace and human security realms. It will be incubating projects whether they are about the application of Big Data for conflict prevention or the exploration of how fear influences peacebuilding from a neuroscience perspective. It might be too early to call peace engineering as the savior of the post-pandemic world, though it is inevitable that it could be pivotal in the realization of a more just and peaceful society. Also, for peace and conflict studies specifically, peace engineering presents a gate to a new world for a more multidisciplinary approach and application to both protracted and new peace and security challenges across the globe.

114 *Alpasian Özerdem and Lisa Schirch*

Notes

1 "Global Humanitarian Overview 2019 – Trends in Humanitarian Needs and Assistance," *Office for the Coordination of Humanitarian Affairs (OCHA)*, November 30, 2018.
2 Carol S. North and Betty Pfefferbaum, "Mental Health and the Covid-19 Pandemic," *The New England Journal of Medicine* 383 (April 13, 2020).
3 Kate Kelland, "U.N. Warns of Global Mental Health Crisis Due to COVID-19 Pandemic," *Reuters*, May 13, 2020.
4 "Social Movement Technologies," https://socialmovementtechnologies.org/.
5 C. Le Quéré et al., "Temporary Reduction in Daily Global CO_2 Emissions During the COVID-19 Forced Confinement," *Nature Climate Change* 10 (2020): 647–653,
6 Susanne Rust, "Bicycles Have Enjoyed a Boom During the Pandemic: Will It Last as Car Traffic Resumes?" *Los Angeles Times*, June 25, 2020.
7 Harvard Business Review, "25 Years Ago I Coined the Phrase 'Triple Bottom Line': Here's Why It's Time to Rethink It," October 23, 2019.
8 Lisa Schirch, "Conflict Assessment and Peacebuilding Planning," https://www.rienner.com/uploads/518a6accde15c.pdf.
9 Tovia Smith, "The Battle Between the Masked and the Masked-Nots Unveils Political Rifts," *National Public Radio*, May 29, 2020.
10 "Climate Change and Covid-19 Increase Pressure on Potable Water Resources," *Sustainability Times*, May 20, 2020, accessed July 1, 2020, www.sustainability-times.com/environmental-protection/climate-change-and-covid-19-increase-pressure-on-potable-water-resources/.
11 Engineering schools around the world are offering new courses and graduate degrees in peace engineering (e.g. Drexel University, University of St. Thomas, University of New Mexico, University of Colorado, University of Texas at El Paso).

13 COVID-19 amidst conflict

Oded Adomi Leshem

Some commentators suggest that in a crisis such as the present global pandemic and recession, a sense of common problems and common goals may help parties long in conflict to develop more peaceful relations. Others insist that a primary effect of the crisis will be to intensify long-held enmities; as fear and insecurity increase, each side is tempted to use the other as a diversion and scapegoat. The author of this chapter uses the insights of social psychology to throw a positive new light on the impact of the pandemic on conflicts in the Holy Land.

Following the outbreak of COVID-19, prominent international figures have called for a global ceasefire. "It is time to put armed conflict on lockdown and focus together on the true fight of our lives," said UN Secretary-General Antonio Guterres. Emmanuel Macron, President of France, announced he is pushing for a "world truce," while other world leaders have offered similar declarations.

Did leaders and citizens involved in violent conflicts heed this call? Did rivals unite to fight the virus instead of each other? Prolonged ethnonational disputes, such as the one in Israel-Palestine, are good places to start examining whether COVID-19 altered the course of violent conflicts. The Jewish and Palestinian national movements have been locked in a hostile dispute for roughly a century. Has the pandemic changed anything in the relationships between these lifelong adversaries?

About fourteen million people, approximately half Jews and half Palestinian, reside between the Jordan River and the Mediterranean Sea in an area of only 28,000km². The high population density makes it an ideal location for quick virus contagion. Indeed, coupled together, Israel and Palestine have the highest rate of confirmed cases per population size in the Middle East (as of June 2020). As elsewhere, fighting COVID-19 has been at the center of attention of Palestinians and Israelis during the spring of 2020. Yet, unlike other places, the two peoples are also engrossed in a violent dispute. What happens when external threats and intergroup conflict combine?

COVID-19 and the mitigation of intergroup conflict

The main point raised by those hoping that the pandemic would have a decisive role in advancing Palestinian–Israeli relations is that a shared goal like fighting the coronavirus would elicit intergroup cooperation and trust. The ability of an external superordinate goal to facilitate conflict resolution was exemplified in the famous Robber's Cave experiment (Sherif 1958).[1] In this study, two groups of boys who, by the design of the researchers, were involved in a hostile competition, reconciled when an external superordinate goal demanded their cooperation. Simply put, when parties to a conflict understand that partnership is vital for overcoming a shared external challenge, they are likely to join forces despite grave animosity. Working together on a shared goal can, in turn, help transform hostile relationships into more cooperative ones. Cooperation creates initial bonds and a feeling of shared destiny that can be later translated to conciliation and peace.

As an external threat of great magnitude, the battle against COVID-19 perfectly fits the definition of a superordinate goal. After all, intergroup cooperation is likely to reduce the risk of contagion of all the residents of the region. Many observers expected that Palestinians and Israelis would team up and, maybe for the first time, work together as real partners. Yet, those waiting for intergroup cooperation overlooked an essential factor. The conflict is asymmetrical, with Israel having much more political, military, and economic power (Bar-Tal 2013; Leshem and Halperin 2020).[2] Extreme disparities in power are unlikely to produce a reciprocal partnership. Indeed, Israel does not need Palestinian technology and knowhow to fight the virus and thus did not pursue cooperation. In fact, the Palestinians' inferior medical infrastructure made them dependent on Israel's kindheartedness – a quality that, to date, has not been extended.

Intergroup cooperation was also not essential for enforcing physical distancing thanks to the 500km-long separation wall that effectively segregates Jews and Palestinians in the West-Bank. The wall, formally erected for security reasons by Israel, made intercommunal contagion improbable. In the besieged Gaza Strip, the 1.9 million Palestinian residents are entirely isolated. Ironically, the Gaza blockade implemented by Israel and Egypt in 2007 has been protecting Gazans from the spread of the deadly virus.

The conflict's asymmetrical nature made intergroup cooperation unlikely. Yet, COVID-19 could have contributed to a more implicit but important positive change in the attitudes of Palestinians and Israelis toward each other. At least potentially, the universalistic nature of the global pandemic can blur existing boundaries between ethnocentric identities by creating a sense of a shared, universalistic identity (Bavel et al., 2020).[3]

We all harbor multiple social identities, some more salient than others. During ethnonational conflicts, ethnocentric identities overshadow universalistic identities that, by their very nature, allude to a connection between groups (Kelman 2018; Rothbart and Korostelina 2006).[4] National and ethnic identities are challenged by global phenomena such as the COVID epidemic. The fact the virus does not discriminate based on race, ethnicity, or religious affiliation may strengthen the sense of universalistic identity at the expense of ethnocentric ones. With the help of the constant flow of reports from around the world, boundaries between groups become obscure, to some degree pointless, and the notion that we are all human beings becomes more apparent. Enhancement of a universalistic identity makes intergroup aggression less likely and may contribute to transforming antagonistic relations into harmonious ones.

Did COVID-19 heighten universalistic identities among Palestinians and Israelis? If this was the case, we should have observed some evidence of intergroup empathy and solidarity in Palestine–Israel (e.g., people trying to reach out to people from the other side, provide consolation and support, and send prayers for the safety of all people). If these processes happened in Israel–Palestine, however, they occurred in the margins. Data collected among 600 Jewish–Israelis at the peak of the COVID crisis shows that more than 60% of did not think COVID brought people of the world together (Adler, Habel, Leshem, and Halperin, in preparation). In addition, most Jewish–Israelis showed little empathetic concerns toward coronavirus-infected Palestinians.

Another point that can be made about the potential of crises like COVID-19 to alleviate conflicts has to do with leadership, or more correctly, with the shift in the source of the power that leaders in conflict-ridden places bank on. For decades, Israeli and Palestinian leaders have attained and maintained power based, almost exclusively, on their image as resolute conflict managers. Yet, during the coronavirus crisis, Palestinian and Israeli leaders could not rely on the conflict as their primary source of power. Citizens' eyes were focused on how their leaders would defeat COVID-19, not their rival from the other side of the border. Did this shift in public attention change the situation on the ground?

In the last decade, the average conflict-related death toll in Israel–Palestine has been around fifty deaths a month, 95% of whom are Palestinian. Yet, between March and May 2020, only twelve people lost their lives due to conflict-related violence (United Nations Office for the Coordination of Humanitarian Affairs).[5] Of course, this drop can also be explained by the change in national priorities. Both parties simply had to reallocate material and human resources from conflict-related endeavors to the battle against the coronavirus.

In short, the shift in national priorities, from managing the conflict to managing the pandemic, has not only changed the allocation of resources but has altered, at least temporarily, the main force propelling Palestinian and Israeli politics. During the spring of 2020, the perpetuation of the conflict ceased to serve leaders' political needs on the domestic front, which might have contributed to the reduction of violence. At least during these months, COVID-19 saved Israelis and Palestinians from killing each other.

Unfortunately, this trend did not last long. When the number of verified cases decreased in late April, intergroup violence raised its head. The most horrific incident happened on May 29, 2020, when Israeli police shot and killed unarmed Iyad al-Halak, a mentally disabled Palestinian resident of East Jerusalem. The killing ignited the all-too-familiar escalation cycle enabling leaders to continue to gain political profits from intergroup violence.

In sum, though COVID-19 could have contributed, at least potentially, to the de-escalation of conflict in Israeli–Palestine, it seems that this potential was left mostly unfulfilled. Intergroup cooperation did not commence, identity boundaries were not blurred, and the temporary hiatus of violence was too short to impact longstanding trends in the politics of the conflict. One would hope that, if things did not get better, at least they would not get worse. Unfortunately, as outlined in the next section, conflict-aggravating processes that emerged during the months of the pandemic were swifter and more profound, thereby aggravating the conflict.

COVID-19 and the aggravation of intergroup conflict

Israel's general elections were held on March 2, several days after the first Israeli virus carriers were confirmed. Partial lockdown was already implemented when the final election results came in. The close match created an impasse, with neither of the two candidates, the incumbent rightwing Benjamin Netanyahu and the novice contender Benny Gantz, able to garner enough parliamentary support to establish a government. Netanyahu announced that fighting the virus demanded unity. Gantz yielded under the pressure and joined Netanyahu's government. Thus, at the peak of the outbreak, an emergency government was hastily formed, enabling Netanyahu to extend his uninterrupted eleven-year reign.

History teaches us that large-scale crises provide the perfect pretense for the suppression of democratic regulations and institutions (Klein 2007).[6] During crises, the public can be is easily led to grant carte blanche to the government to do as it sees fit. This is what happened with one of the first decisions of Israel's new emergency government. Without public outcry,

Israel's government authorized the Shin Bet (Israeli's Security Agency) and the Mossad (the National Intelligence Agency) to head some of the efforts of the fight against COVID-19. Expanding the jurisdiction of these two security agencies to non-security issues is one factor that may have drastic consequences on the post-corona era in Israel–Palestine.

Netanyahu's track record in the field of Israeli–Palestinian relations suggests that his continued rule is likely to result in yet another set of blows to Palestinian–Israeli peace. Since 2009, his governments have not only been antagonistic to the notion of peace but also have actively fought to remove peace from the country's agenda. During his incumbency, the rate of illegal construction of Jewish settlements in the West Bank peaked, violence against Palestinians spurred, and racist sentiments against the 1.8 million Palestinian citizens of Israel reached new heights. By providing a guise for an emergency government, the health crisis has enabled the continuation of an extremely hardline administration.

Another point worth mentioning is that besides the severe ramifications to global health, the coronavirus outbreak ravaged the livelihoods of many. From the standstill in the flow of goods to the skyrocketing levels of unemployment, peoples' ontological security has been threatened. The longevity of the crisis and the scope of its destruction leave people anxious and stressed. With no immunization in sight, uncertainty has become the only thing certain.

During conflict, uncertainty and anxiety from an external threat could be conveniently redirected at the hated rival. Relative to the amorphic and faceless virus, the outgroup is a familiar and recognizable enemy. Venting tensions and scapegoating are more likely when governments fail to deal with ontological threats. When the government's inability to protect the public is exposed, citizens and elites will look for a scapegoat. For Israelis and Palestinians, the lifelong enemy across the border is a convenient scapegoat. It is, therefore, quite possible that a second wave of COVID-19 could be followed by violence. Intergroup confrontations could deflect citizens' criticism against their leaders' ill-management of the crisis and might, quite ironically, restore Israelis' and Palestinians' sense of certainty and predictability (Leshem and Halperin In Press).[7]

Cautious speculations

As I write these lines, only three months into the COVID crisis, it is hard to tell where the wind is blowing. COVID-19 is still taking its toll in the region and its total economic ramifications are unclear. Yet, very cautiously, I can try to identify two possible scenarios that may unfold in Palestine–Israel in the post-COVID-19 era.

The first is the "more of the same" scenario, namely, the gradual but systematic destruction of hope for a just and sustainable solution to the conflict in Israel–Palestine. Palestinians will continue to live under oppression and Jewish–Israelis will remain unsecure east and west of the Green Line even after the virus will be long gone. This prediction draws on the "intractable conflict" paradigm, which holds that, though fluctuating in intensity, intractable conflicts are remarkably stable (Coleman et al. 2007; Bar-Tal 2013).[8] The second option is that COVID-19 will serve as a catalyst expediting a large-scale breakdown in the region, which will include the collapse of democracy in Israel, full-fledged confrontations between Israel and the Palestinians on several fronts, the annulment of Israel's treaties with Egypt and Jordan, and regional instability.

Some place for optimism?

Did COVID-19 have any positive influence on the relationship between Jews and Palestinians, influences that are substantial and not only superficial or transient? Amid mostly negative processes, I wish to highlight one positive consequence in my concluding remarks.

Palestinian citizens of Israel (who also identify as "Israeli Arabs" or "Arabs of 48"), make up about 20% of Israeli citizenry. In the last decades, two simultaneous processes concerning their social and political status should be noted. On the one hand, state-sanctioned discrimination and popular racism against Palestinian citizens of Israel have been on the rise (Ghanem 2007).[9] Israeli legislators have passed discriminatory laws aimed at limiting their power and sense of collective identity while anti-Arab and anti-Muslim sentiments have become more open and frequent in the public discourse. On the other hand, the presence of Palestinian citizens of Israel in the public landscape has increased. In the universities, in the general workforce, in the media, the existence of Palestinian citizens of Israel could no longer be ignored by the Jewish majority. Gradually, their calls for equality and fair opportunity have become more evident. Their demand, as Palestinian Arabs, to take an active part in shaping the future of the state has become more decisive.

The necessity to see Palestinian citizens of Israel as an integral, indispensable part of the Israeli collective was made clear during the coronavirus outbreak, when thousands of Arab medical personnel, doctors, nurses, and technicians, took an active part in battling COVID-19. Up until then, it was convenient for the Jewish majority to ignore the Palestinian community's contribution to the state. This all changed in the three months of the outbreak as medical teams led by Arab and Jewish physicians worked day and night to save lives.

Images and stories of Jews and Arabs working side by side were broadcast on national media outlets. Social media campaigns saluting the heroic efforts of Arab doctors have also gained attention. The once extremely unpopular notion of Arab–Jewish partnership became acceptable, even desirable, among the Jewish majority. It is not that racism disappeared from public discourse. Yet, maybe for the first time, it had a powerful rival.

Being Palestinian by ethnicity and Israeli by citizenship, Palestinian citizens of Israel are likely to have a leading role in any advancement toward an agreement on the status of the Occupied Palestinian Territories (Levy et al. 2017).[10] The rise in their involvement, voice, and legitimacy during the coronavirus crisis could evolve to be the first step in the direction of peace for all those living between the River and the Sea.

Notes

1 Muzafer Sherif, "Superordinate Goals in the Reduction of Intergroup Conflict," *American Journal of Sociology* (1958): 349–56.
2 Daniel Bar-Tal, *Intractable Conflicts* (Cambridge: Cambridge University Press, 2013).
3 Jay J. Van Bavel, Katherine Baicker, Paulo S. Boggio, Valerio Capraro, Aleksandra Cichocka, Mina Cikara, Molly J. Crockett et al., "Using Social and Behavioural Science to Support COVID-19 Pandemic Response," *Nature Human Behaviour* 4, no. 5 (2020): 460–71, https://doi.org/10.1038/s41562-020-0884-z.
4 Daniel Rothbart and K. V. Korostelina, *Identity, Morality, and Threat: Studies in Violent Conflict* (Lanham: Lexington Books, 2006), http://public.ebookcentral. proquest.com/choice/publicfullrecord.aspx?p=1331624; Herbert C. Kelman, *Transforming the Israeli-Palestinian Conflict: From Mutual Negation to Reconciliation*, ed. Philip Matter and Neil Caplan (Abingdon, Oxon: Routledge, 2018).
5 "Data on Casualties – United Nations Office for the Coordination of Humanitarian Affairs," *United Nations Office for the Coordination of Humanitarian Affairs – Occupied Palestinian Territory*, n.d., accessed May 19, 2019, www. ochaopt.org/data/casualties.
6 Naomi Klein, *The Shock Doctrine: The Rise of Disaster Capitalism* (New York: Metropolitan Books Holt, 2007).
7 Oded Adomi Leshem and Eran Halperin, "Hope During Conflict," in *Historical and Multidisciplinary Perspectives on Hope*, ed. Steven Van den Heuvel (Springer, In Press); Oded Adomi Leshem and Eran Halperin, "Hoping for Peace During Protracted Conflict: Citizens' Hope Is Based on Inaccurate Appraisals of Their Adversary's Hope for Peace," *Journal of Conflict Resolution* 28 (2020).
8 Peter T. Coleman, Robin R. Vallacher, Andrzej Nowak, and Lan Bui-Wrzosinska, "Intractable Conflict as an Attractor a Dynamical Systems Approach to Conflict Escalation and Intractability," *American Behavioral Scientist* 50, no. 11 (2007): 1454–75, doi:10.1177/0002764207302463.

9 As'ad Ghanem, "Israel and the 'Danger of Demography'," in *Where Now for Palestine? The Demise of the Two-State Solution*, ed. Jamil Hilal, 48–74 (London: Zed, 2007).
10 Aharon Levy, Tamar Saguy, Martijn van Zomeren, and Eran Halperin, "Ingroups, Outgroups, and the Gateway Groups Between: The Potential of Dual Identities to Improve Intergroup Relations," *Journal of Experimental Social Psychology* 70 (May 2017): 260–71, https://doi.org/10.1016/j.jesp.2016.09.011.

14 When elephants roar

The coming moral conflict between the United States and China

Gao Qing

An immediate consequence of the COVID-19 pandemic has been a worsening of relations between the United States and China on several fronts, including diplomacy, trade, and military competition in East Asia. Are the two great powers on the same path to escalated conflict that generated two world wars in the twentieth century? This essay by a leading figure in the Confucius Institute describes the likely impact of a period of extended and uneven economic recovery on their relations, emphasizing steps that groups interested in conflict resolution can take to turn these possible scenarios in a more peaceful direction.

When Dr. Henry Kissinger recalled his first meeting with Premier Minister Chou En-lai during his secret trip to China on July 9, 1971, he wrote,

> *I had prepared a long and slightly pedantic opening statement, reciting the history of US-Chinese relations that had led up to the present meeting. At the end of its introductory part I said with an attempt at eloquence: "Many visitors have come to this beautiful, and to us, mysterious land." Chou [En-lai] held up his hand: "You will find it not mysterious. When you have become familiar with it, it will not be as mysterious as before." I was taken aback, but Chou was certainly right. Our concern was not the bilateral issues between us – at least at first. We had to build confidence; to remove the mystery. (Kissinger 1979)*

Since then, a structure of complex multidimensional bilateral relations between the United States and China has served as an anchor of regional stability and global economic development, which as Kissinger anticipated, has become "one of the foundations of contemporary international relations," particularly in the post-Cold War era. Nearly forty-nine years later, however, we find ourselves standing at a historical crossroad with confusion, frustration, and anxiety characterizing the uncertainty of US-China relations. In 1971, it was crucial for the United States and China to developing a working partnership. Today the problem is existential. When Kissinger and Chou came to know one another, China remained a sleepy giant at the frontier of modernity. Today, it is as much a rival principle to the West itself as it is an economic behemoth. If there is one relationship in the world that is essential for the future of human flourishing all around the world, it is that between the United States and China. The myopic and confrontation reaction of the two countries to it might impede a healthy conversation between them, which makes it all the more critical for the field to invest in conflict resolution theory and practice with respect to this most central of all bilateral relationships.

Between the United States and China: a new cold war?

Since the normalization of US-China diplomatic relations, a range of contentious issues raised by both sides has continued to unfold in geopolitics, trade and economy, ideology and social values, civil rights and state governance, and in technology. Those issues reflect both sharp and subtle differences which have emerged and evolved over a relatively long time span. Nevertheless, these various contentions and confrontations can be characterized as part of single *complex of strained cooperation*. This complex, in my view, can be viewed from four perspectives.

First, the developing relationship between the two countries across a multitude of fields has proven to be *mutually* productive and beneficial, overshadowing the contentions and hostilities that have divided the countries. China's engagement with the United States, as well as its integration into the international community with policy of openness, has greatly improved Chinese standards of living, infrastructure and industrial modernization, education, and technology, while the United States has benefited from access to the largest market in world history and the import of affordable products. China's strong and stable economic performance during the 2008 financial recession in particular anchored the bumpy financial market in the United States and elsewhere. Although issues related to intellectual property and technology transfers have raised accusations and blame from both sides, joint ventures, collaborations, and investments have contributed to rapid technological development and innovation both in Silicon Valley, California and Zhongguancun, Beijing.

Second, the international community has been explicitly and overwhelmingly in favor of a stable US–China bilateral relationship, as opposed to the toxic versions that now threaten to emerge. The rapid growth of China, benefited by economic engagement and connections with the United States, has become the largest engine of global economic growth since 2008 for the world as a whole. In the recent decade, the ties and cooperation between the United States and China have shaped international joint forces to address pressing global problems, including nuclear weapon proliferation, regional armed conflict prevention, disaster relief, international crime, climate change, energy sustainability, global poverty, and, ironically, global diseases and pandemic (Swaine 2019). To thoughtful international observers, the coincidence of competition and cooperation was a dynamic that was good for the world itself, whatever its drawbacks.

Third, the issues and incidents throughout the twentieth century that halted or set back the progress of the bilateral relationship were almost all *mono*-directional in the sense that all the action was in the vicinity of China itself. In the first thirty years of diplomatic relations, the United States has consistently been in the position of raising dissatisfactions and initiating pressures toward China in locales in or near China and far away from the United States, such as Korea, Japan, Vietnam, and Taiwan. This reflected the unbalanced power and influence between the two sides and the relatively weak position of China in those years. The good news is that as China has grown in strength, it has pressed for a gradual evolution of the balance of power despite its own revolutionary origins. This evolutionary attitude is now a stable feature of Chinese global policy.

Fourth, the core of policymakers and social elites on both sides have consistently engaged in prudent and effective maneuvers to navigate through the various episodes of bilateral turbulence that could have disrupted global stability during the critical moments of the evolving relationship. From the establishment of Pakistan Channel for secretly connecting the top leaders between the two countries, to the Hainan Island incident of 2001 in which a US Navy EP-3 signals intelligence aircraft collided with China's People's Liberation Army J-8 interceptor fighter, decision-makers have carefully conducted restrained measures to prevent direct conflicts. This prudence has become a relatively stable feature of the complex of strained US–China cooperation.

As promising as this complex may be, current trends are clearly signaling a different direction as the relationship continues to move toward a more dangerous level of confrontation and animosity. These portents of a new and perhaps even more dangerous Cold War have left analysts of US–China relations trained in international relations desperate to use their limited diplomatic options and measures to repair the broken relationship. Many of these analysts, however, are stuck in a twentieth century mentality, upholding the immediate unilateral interests of their own nation and attempting to intimidate the other side into making concessions. To maintain global stability and prevent disastrous direct conflicts between the two essential nations, we need a new way of thinking. This is why it is so critical for the field of peace and conflict resolution to center its efforts on the future of the

US/China relationship, something which has yet to be done on an adequate scale.

Deconstructing the rising power myth

It is true that much of the most intense conflict in the latter part of the twentieth century, from Korea and Vietnam to the South China Sea, can be thought of as a competitive struggle between the United States and China, and yet a deeper analysis reveals the existence of a complex of strained stability. What, then, led both sides to become poised toward a state of conflict? One perspective frequently noted is summarized in Graham Allison's term, the Thucydides Trap: a rising power rivals the existing supremacy of an established power in ways that can only be resolved through military confrontation. Unfortunately, this pattern fails to recognize the deep roots of this conflict in both parties' domestic politics and projected histories. Despite hawkish and hostile narratives, the stability complex that has evolved to contain the hostilities of the two sides suggests that the true interests of the two nations are far from incompatible.

Part of the problem is that the recent history of global power has biased our attention toward the West. We have paid excess attention to the interests, ideas, and foibles of the United States, as if Chinese domestic concerns and historical memory were irrelevant. The social identity of the Chinese people and the likely effects of the crisis on them is much less well understood. China's long and vibrant ancient history and the dramatic social changes in the modern and contemporary periods are only now beginning to be investigated with proper theoretical frames to ground the research.

Among the most useful conflict resolution tools available to gain access to Chinese, social identity is the well-known concept of "chosen trauma" developed by the psychoanalyst Vamik Volkan (Volkan 1991, 2001). Chinese modernity has been haunted by its experience of the nineteenth century. From the first Opium War in 1840 to the founding of the People's Republic of China is a period commonly referred to in China as "one hundred years of humiliation," a phrase demonstrating how the Chinese people see themselves as having been victimized by Western oppressors. The suspicion and resentment generated by this historical memory frames the view of the West, both past and present, and much anti-Western rhetoric derives from suspicion that criticism of China is little more than an attempt to curb the recent rise of the nation and is intended to bring back suffering and hardships to the Chinese people.

But not all views of how the West came east are negative or destructive of Chinese self-confidence. Two other sentiments related to the experience of historical trauma frame the typical Chinese self-concept as well. First is the admiration of modern science and technology whose superiority was clearly demonstrated by national humiliations. The public consensus in China ascribes China's defeat by Western forces during much of the modern era to a mismatch between the two sides in science and technological capacity, a product of the Industrial Revolution. Joseph Stalin's proclamation of "those who fall behind get beaten" has been very well received in China and is probably a more popular phrase there than in the original country. Views like these have motivated Chinese society to focus on the development of science, technology, and engineering to quickly catch up with the pace in the industrial countries. It has forged a mindset that China has the historical duty and right to acquire new technology regardless of the obstacles that others may put in the way and pride in recent progress on this account forms a key part of Chinese self-confidence today. For better relations in the future, Western leaders should recognize the importance to the Chinese self-concept of this drive to acquire Western techniques. It will not be readily conceded, no matter how strident the accusations of intellectual property theft may become. Therefore, intellectual property arguments should always be understood in this interpretive context.

The second point is related to the first. The depth and long endurance of the mismatch of science and technology between East and West has produced a tendency to lionize Western technological superiority even if the West is still seen as spiritually backward. This sentiment has motived great efforts across almost all disciplines of Chinese educational institutions to imitate and reproduce the Western model of higher education, promoting educational exchanges on a vast scale that may well be one of the signal features of intellectual development of the twenty-first century. The pandemic has disrupted this historic flow of students and ideas, but it will change its form rather than putting an end to it. Success in higher education and technological development has bolstered Chinese social identity just as American superiority has been perceived to decline. As the American domestic economy faltered after the Great Recession in 2008, and as issues of social injustice have come to the fore, China has returned to a much older story to explain itself: that of the old "middle kingdom" that now sits at the middle of the whole world, a state with an obligation to serve the world as well as a claim to preeminence. Most recently, the comparison of the efficiency of government measures against the pandemic by China and the United States has reinforced that confidence and led to a perception that "China's systematic advantage" will continually outperform the West.

This volatile mix of views of history and destiny leaves China in a complex relationship with the new world order created under Western leadership after World War II. In some sense, China should be thought of not as joining the existing system as much as providing an opportunity to reimagine it, a condition demanded by the inexorable fact of Chinese growth. China's successful growth has been largely due to the pragmatism and realistic mentality that Deng Xiaoping decisively introduced on his watch to mediate various contradictory opinions regarding the direction of the nation. The unquestioned success of that attitude continues to drive Chinese policymakers in their statecraft. Deng's famous metaphor, "whether a cat is black or white, a cat that can catch rats is a good cat" illustrated his view of prioritizing tangible and substantial development over ideological purity. This attitude provides an opportunity for a realistic engagement of China and the West as they emerge from the pandemic, but it has also led to rampant materialism in Chinese society and also to an overconfidence that could become an obstacle to effective dialogue in addressing issues and building trust to prevent conflict escalation.

East and West after the Pandemic

Although there is little in the first thirty years of bilateral diplomatic relations to suggest that tensions between China and the United States will soon abate, it is critical to remember that US–China interaction is not merely about these two countries. As the two largest economies from two sides of the Pacific Ocean, this relationship impacts everywhere in the globe. Unlike the Cold War, however, when two camps were divided by the ideological differences, it will be nearly impossible for most countries to choose sides in this relationship. Economic relations with both China and the United States are crucial, and for most of the countries, there is insufficient direct hostility toward either side sufficient to prompt conflict and a Cold War style division.

In addition, the challenges of establishing regional security and stability around the world will very likely lead to more pragmatic engagements between the United States and China in global governance. The European Union has been a powerful example of cooperation sufficient to balance the influence of both the United States and China. Each side needs to take to interests of a newly united Europe more seriously than it did before. Other multilateral structures such as the Arab League, the African Union, and the Association of Southeast Asian Nations are likely to grow in independence and strength, while countries in Latin America and even East Asia may be more motivated to consider closer patterns of regional integration. This change, if it occurs, will drastically change the landscape of global order by further diminishing unipolar supremacy, providing a more flexible mechanism for dealing with regional and international conflicts and mitigating the East–West divide.

The field of peace and conflict resolution provides us with many of the tools we need to confront the challenge of a new world order that will arise after the pandemic. The field and its concepts help us to recognize the role of culture in each conflict situation, the burdens of history, and the frameworks through which new experiences are interpreted. Those who recognize the gaps in culture, history, and interpretation between the United States and China will know how to better conduct future peacebuilding initiatives between the two leading powers of the coming century. Instead of the dire warnings of a Thucydides Trap that condemns the two to animosity and struggle, trends supporting mutual learning across cultural divides may create an opportunity to form an authentic and healthy relationship between people east and west based on empathy, respect, and appreciation of cross-cultural human experience. The sense of humanity and universal values of peace, justice and yes, even love, are the fundamental components of every culture, which can become a bridge of solidarity to bring people together.

References

Bell, Daniel A., and Pei Wang. *Just Hierarchy: Why Social Hierarchies Matter in China. and the Rest of the World*. Princeton, NJ: Princeton University Press, 2020.

Cheung, Chantai. "The New Yellow Peril? – Anti-Chinese Sentiment in the West." *Northeastern University Political Review*, March 18, 2020. www.nupoliticalreview. com/2020/03/18/the-new-yellow-peril-anti-chinese-sentiment-in-the-west/.

Ferguson, Niall. "We're All State Capitalists Now." *Foreign Policy*, 2012. https:// foreignpolicy.com/2012/02/09/were-all-state-capitalists-now/.

Galtung, Johan. *Solving Conflicts: A Peace Research Perspective*. Honolulu: University of Hawaii Press, 1989.

Kissinger, A. Henry. *White House Years*. Boston: Little Brown, 1979.

Lederach, John P. *Building Peace: Sustainable Reconciliation in Divided Society*. Washington, DC: United States Institute of Peace Press, 1997.

Miall, Hugh, Oliver Ramsbotham, and Tom Woodhouse. *Contemporary Conflict Resolution*. Cambridge: Polity, 1999.

———. *Open Doors*. Institution of International Education, 2019. https://iiebooks. stores.yahoo.net/opdoreonined.html.

Rubenstein, E. Richard. *Reasons to Kill: Why Americans Choose War*. New York: Bloomsbury Press, 2010.

Swaine, D. Michael. "A Relationship Under Extreme Duress: U.S.-China Relations at a Crossroads." *Carnegie Endowment for International Peace*, January 16, 2019. https://carnegieendowment.org/2019/01/16/relationship-under-extreme-duress-u.s.-china-relations-at-crossroads-pub-78159.

Volkan, Vamid D. "On Chosen Trauma." *Mind and Human Interaction* 4 (1991): 3–19.

———. "Transgenerational Transmissions and Chosen Traumas: An Aspect of Large-Group Identity." *Group Analysis* 34, no. 1 (2001): 79–97.

Concluding note

Solon Simmons and Richard E. Rubenstein

In early March 2020, the director of the National Institute of Allergy and Infectious Diseases and world expert on infectious diseases, Dr. Anthony Fauci, gave an interview about the novel corona virus in which he said, "I don't think that we are going to get out of this completely unscathed . . . I think that this is going to be one of those things we look back on and say boy, that was bad.[1]" What Fauci could see in the future we can all see now in our present. Boy, the global pandemic has been bad, and we are still unaware of the full extent of its effects. In this volume, we have attempted to speculate about what the range of those effects has been, looking over the terrain of peace and conflict studies with an eye to providing rough forecasts in specific areas drawn from the varied forms of expertise assembled in this volume. What might happen in the space of peacebuilding and conflict resolution, what challenges, what complications, what reasons for despair, and what bases for hope?

As peacemakers, we feel obligated to err a bit on the side of hope but have worked with the small community of scholar/practitioners assembled here to channel that hope in realistic directions, given the scale of the tragedy unfolding before us. The short essays collected here cover a range of concerns typical in the field, from questions of social justice to great power relations and global hotspots, but throughout, the focus remains on a central tension implicit in the subtitle of the book, that between building peace and pursuing justice. Each of the authors struggles with the implications of a less than obvious yet inherent tension between these very practical goals of justice and peace, one stressing the wrongs of the past and their lingering force in the present, and the other the hope for the future and those innocents unfairly condemned to bear the consequences of our mistakes. Those prioritizing justice favor speaking truth to power even in the face of adversity, while those focused on peace emphasize finding common ground even with those who are most odious to us. This tension and its divisive implications are something that we in the peace and conflict field need to make much more of. In fact, the peace scholar John Paul Lederach made this tension a centerpiece of his vision of the field in a provocative essay, "Justpeace: The Challenge of the 21st Century," which he later defined as a process that decreased violence and increased justice at the same time.[2]

Promising as the convergence of the concepts of peace and justice sounds, it becomes increasingly clear that skills and strategies best suited to pursue justice are quite different and sometimes even directly opposed to the skills and strategies conducive to building peace. The former most often requires community mobilization, clarity of purpose, attention to the past, sharp distinctions between right and wrong, competitive strategy, and what Congressman John Lewis called, "good trouble.[3]" The latter is best served by public de-escalation, immersion in complexity, emphasis on the future, moral humility, a cooperative attitude, and what peace scholar, Howard Zehr has called "restorative practices."[4] As movements that predate the pandemic like #Blacklivesmatter and other anti-racism initiatives have shown, the practice of peace and the practice of justice can be as much at odds as complementary. It is hard for mass publics to maintain a restorative attitude in the face of global disarray, failed leadership, and a continuation of historic injustices. Things only become more complicated as society becomes infused with the varied and contradictory master narratives that once defined the separate spheres of human activity. One person's version of overcoming of injustice is often the other person's version of abuse of power, and the people best suited to getting an issue to the table may not the ones best suited to negotiating at the table. The goals of peace and justice can work together, but the essays presented here demonstrate the weight of the burden on conflict specialists to manage this founding tension of the field, pursuing justice as we build peace at the same time.

The contributors to this book make clear how conflict resolution after the pandemic will be further complicated by the size, scope, and complexity of the problems posed by the coronavirus plague. History teaches us that outbreaks of disease seldom change the world on their own but do accelerate processes already underway. For example, several of our authors suggest that the world order that came into existence at the end of the Cold War – an arrangement featuring a globally hegemonic United States supported by European and Japanese junior partners – will very likely give way to a more complex and multifaceted system, one in which the United States and Europe play important, but less dominant roles. What the new world system looks like is hard to predict in specific terms, but we can be sure that it will be more diverse in the range of cultural traditions on which it builds and will need to speak a language more inclusive than that used even by the aspirational leaders who established the Universal Declaration of Human Rights in 1948.[5]

Most important, it will become essential for those who hope to build peace while pursuing justice to better develop their imaginations as they apply to questions of economic justice and economic democracy. Whatever else the coming world order will bring, it will very likely involve negotiating a new or revised set of arrangements for the production, exchange, and distribution of goods and services, as well as a new set or relationships between public and private authorities. Rather than merely hiring neoliberal economists or international development specialists to apply existing knowledge in peacebuilding projects, the essays collected here suggest the need to cultivate new areas in the political economy of the world system, including a network of scholars and activists who can clearly point out how the current configuration of global capitalism leads to inequalities, ruptured identities, environmental degradation, and ultimately, the erosion of democratic politics itself.

The big peace movements of the early twentieth century never shied away from these questions of political economy. It is time that those of us who grew up in the shadow of the Cold War get over our own fears of ideological polarization and anxieties about our tendencies to innumeracy in order to bring fresh perspectives to a series of interrelated festering problems.[6] As Thomas Piketty has argued, one can think about economics without subscribing to fantasy abstractions that have little bearing on how businesses are run or international agreements are negotiated, relying instead on the techniques of empirical social science both quantitative and qualitative.[7]

This last point, which we might label the question of capitalism, runs through this volume in some ways clear and some ways hidden. It seems fair to say that those of us in the field of peace and conflict studies feel more comfortable speaking about ethnicity than we do economy, colonialization than capital, but even so, we all know that each of the conflicts we study can be fitted into some larger pattern of social evolution that has something to do with the intersection of money and power. Even the most strident critics of what has been called the neoliberal peace seem to shy away from this question of capitalism itself, the very engine that runs the world, perhaps for fear of seeming too radical or even naïve. But the very scale of the tragedy of the pandemic, especially if it is part of an Anthropocene transformation that will bring along changes in climate like those already on display, will force those of us who care about peace and justice to enter into economic affairs from the perspective of morality and justice.

As many of us have noticed, interest in conflict resolution has become worldwide, and the pandemic will only drive that interest, while people increasingly wonder what kind of peace comes after this unmistakable turning point. Those interested in peacebuilding will therefore find themselves consulting philosophers of history and society like Giovanni Arrighi, whose magisterial sociological history describes the mechanisms and cycles of stages of accumulation in the development of the world system, beginning in the fourteenth century.[8] World capitalism never ended in communist revolution and is not likely to do so now, but it was integrated into a broader institutional arena in which moral conversations and institutional constraints played a critical role. What the next step in this development will be will depend upon a conversation that is just beginning, but in which conflict and peace scholars can play a creative facilitative role.

As we expand our imaginations and embolden our practice, we will have to keep in mind a central tension for the field – that between pursuing justice and building peace. This tension will force us to engage in a wider set of considerations that touches on social movements and adversarial politics, drawing us directly into the space of disciplines not traditionally associated with peacemaking and conflict resolution. As the world reels, buffeted by disease coupled with a democracy deficit playing out even in the core of the world system, peacemaking seems as much a necessity for the world's most privileged and powerful nations as for those sometimes denigrated as "failed" or "failing" states. One prediction we feel quite confident to make is that the pandemic will only increase the demand for a "justpeace" and those who know how to build it.

Notes

1 " 'You Don't Want to Go to War with a President'," https://www.politico.com/news/2020/03/03/anthony-fauci-trump-coronavirus-crisis-118961.
2 John Paul Lederach, "Justpeace – the Challenge of the 21st Century," www.masstrails.com/mrap/wp-content/uploads/2016/11/Peace-Building-Theoretical-and-Concrete-Perspectives-LitReview.pdf; Lederach, *The Moral Imagination.*
3 Lewis and D'Orso, *Walking with the Wind.*
4 Zehr, *The Little Book of Restorative Justice.*
5 Glendon, *A World Made New.*
6 Gittings, *The Glorious Art of Peace.*
7 Piketty, "Capital in the 21st Century."
8 Giovanni Arrigh, *The Long Twentieth Century: Money, Power, and the Origin of Our Times* (London: Verso, 2010). Other thinkers whom peace and conflict scholars may want to study include Immanuel Wallerstein, Samir Amin, and the fourteenth century Arab philosopher, Ibn Khaldun.

Index

Abbas, Mousavi 64
access to information 11
Addams, Jane 12
advocacy 36, 39
Africa 91
African Americans 38, 76, 81
African Union 128
agriculture/agricultural 26–9, 111
AIDS 19
alcohol/AA 110
Algeria 37–9
al-Halak, Iyad 118
Alternative für Deutschland 46
Altmaier, Peter 63
American White Evangelical
    Protestants (WEP) 97–103
Amnesty's Refugees and Migrants
    Rights 92–3
Angell, Norman 12
anti-globalization 53
anti-hate speech movement 48
anti-racist 5, 82
anxiety 56, 68, 108, 110, 119, 123
Arab League 128
Arab Spring/uprising 36, 73
Arbery, Ahmaud 76
Arden, Jacinda 94
Arrighi, Giovanni 132
Asians 18, 56
Association of Southeast Asian
    Nations 128
asylum-seekers see migration
Atlanta 39
Australia 19, 44

Bassel Al-Assad International Airport 64
BC/AC (Before Corona/After Corona)
    61, 66–7
Beirut 37
Belarus 39
Big Data/big data 109, 112
big peace 5, 9, 11–15, 132
biomedical 5, 17, 24, 51, 73–6, 107
Black Death 18–20, 38, 40
#Blacklivesmatter 131
Black people 82–3, 85–6
Blow, Charles M. 76
Bolivia 37
Bolsonaro, Jair 94
Boutros-Ghali, Boutros 11
Brazil 3, 39, 41, 55–6, 66, 94
Bremmer, Ian 64
Briggs, Charles A. 99
British 10, 65
Burton, John 67
Byrne, Iain 92

cacerolazo 39
Cairo 37
Canada 28, 56
capitalism 27, 77, 82, 98, 132–3
carbon emissions/contributions
    27–9, 110
Carter School Peace Labs (GMU) 113
Chadwick, Edwin 20
Chapel Hill 40
Charlottesville riot 3
Cherkaoui, Mohammed 61
child marriage 92, 95

Chile 36–9
China 3, 5, 20, 27, 38, 52, 54, 56,
    62–3, 65–6, 75, 89, 91, 123–9
China's People's Liberation Army 125
cholera 18, 20
Christians 98–*99*
civil liberties 51, 55, 57
civil rights: activists 83–4; movement
    20–1, 81, 124
class struggle 5
climate change 1, 2, 4, 22, 29, 45, 63, 98
Cold War 9, 13, 62, 123–5, 128, 131–2
Coletivo Rapo Reto 39
colonialism 61, 82, 108
Conference on Peace in Libya 64
conflict analysis and resolution
    (field of) 2
conflict prevention 27, 109, 113, 125
conflict *response* 26–7
Confucius Institute 123
Coordinadora 8M 39
coronavirus: climate 25; economic
    17, 21
Coronavirus Task Force 94
counternarrative 48
Cremer, William 12
crisis 24–5, 28, 30, 107–8, 110, 113,
    125, 132; activists 39; denial; 98;
    political 101; refugees 26–7
culture-and-conflict 27
CureVac 63

Dabney, Robert L. 98
Davidson, Charles 97
Declaration on the Commemoration of
    the Seventy-Fifth Anniversary of the
    United Nations 66
Defend Black Lives 110
"defund the police" 13
dehumanization 56
delegitimization of governance systems 2
demilitarizing 79, 84
Democrats 54, 113
demonstrations 1, 3, 17, 40, 75, 81–2
Denmark 57
Department of Homeland Security 56
diplomacy 62, 79, 123
diplomatic 64–5, 124–5, 128
disarmament 114

discrimination 56, 120
doctors 12, 89, 120–1
Douglas, Mary 100

East–West divide 128
Ebola 52, 91
economics, regenerative 28
ecosystems 28
Educational Engineering Societies
    (IFEES) 107
elections 13, 37, 79, 118
elites 3, 53–5, 57, 119, 125
emissions, carbon 26, 29, 110
English, Michael 73
En-lai, Chou 123–4
environmental 3–4, 24, 26–8, 30, 79,
    108–9, 132
Estonia 65
Euro-Mediterranean 43
European Union/EU 44, 51, 54, 57, 128

factory-farmed 27, 29
fake news 39, 99
family 27, 89, 94
farms/farmers 1, 24, 25, 27–9, 58, 111
fascism 53, 79; neofascism 79
Fauci, Dr. Anthony 101, 130
feudalism 38, 61
Floyd, George 39, 76, 82–3, 86
food: policy 28, 90; production 27, 81,
    111; scarcity 26, 39, 89, 92; security
    26; sustainability 24; systems 25,
    27–30
foreign aid 53
Foreign Direct Investment 44
fossil fuels 24–9
France 36, 37, 40, 65, 92, 115
Fraser, Nancy 14
Fried, Alfred 12
Fukuyama, Francis 52, 62

Gantz, Benny 118
Gautam, Neelam K. 89
gender 14, 78, 89–90, 92–5, 113
genocide 77
*Geopolitical Outlook of the Gulf Crisis
    Trajectory, A* 64
Georgetown University 66
Gezi Park 37

Ghebreyesus, Dr. Tedros 65
globalization 35–6, 40, 47, 52–4,
    61, 74
Globalization 2.0 67
Global South 12, 55
Gostin, Lawrence O. 66
Graham, Allison 126
Great Depression 1, 21–2, 75
Grech, Omar 43
Group of Four (G-4) 66
Gurr, Ted R. 22
Guterres, António 65, 68, 115
"G-Zero world" 64

Habermas, Jürgen 57
health: facilities 94; insurance 94;
    private 2; public 2; strategies 13, 19
Health Silk Road 62
Hillbilly Elegy (Vance) 103
Hmeimim Air Base 64
Hong Kong 36–8
hot spots 74
Hotze, Steve 99
Houthis 65
Howard-Browne, Rodney 99
humanitarian 65, 108; aid 14, 93, 109
human rights 9, 11, 13, 43–4, 46–8,
    56–8, 112
human trafficking 11
Hungary 55–6
Hydroxychloroquine 66

immigrants 52–3, 78; *see also*
    migrants
immunization 19
India 3, 20, 40, 55–6, 66, 94
industrialized nations 29
Industrial Revolution 61, 127
inequality 1–2, 4, 17, 57, 73, 76, 78,
    83, 107
infringement of liberty 75
Ing-wen, Tsai 94
innovations 18, 38, 124
intergroup conflicts 4–5, 107, 116–19
International Criminal Court 63
International Labour Organization 45
International Monetary Fund 75
international relations 5, 11–12, 53, 61,
    123, 125

international trade 20, 35–6, 40, 48, 53,
    58, 62, 64, 123–4
Iran 36–7, 52, 64
Islam 55
Israel 55, 64, 115–21
Israel-Palestine 115; *see also* Palestine/
    Palestinians
Istanbul 37

Jafari, Sheherazade 89
Jew/Jewish 18, 115–17, 119–21
Jia, Qingguo 62–3
jobs 1, 28, 30, 45, 46, 55–7, 68, 76, 81,
    84, 90, 92
Johns Hopkins University 62
Joint Comprehensive Plan of Action 63
justice: 12–13, 16, 28–29, 36, 48,
    74, 76, 79, 129–33; economic 53,
    73; racial 3, 21, 26, 77, 81–83, 86;
    restorative 85; social 25–27, 35,
    37–41, 47, 76, 79, 108, 127
"Justpeace" 131, 133

Kant, Immanuel 67
Kellogg-Briand Peace Pact 11
Kiev 37
Kissinger, Henry 62, 123
Korostelina, Karina V. 51
Kremlin 65; *see also* Russia
Kropotkin, Peter 22

LaFayette, Bernard 84
Latakia 64
Latinxs 81
Lebanon 36–9
Lederach, John P. 84, 93, 131
Leshem, Oded A. 115–17, 119
Lewis, John 131
lockdown 37, 55–7, 68, 74–5, 78, 89,
    92–3, 110, 118
low-income communities 25, 28–9
Lukashenko, Alexander 39
Lyons, Terrence 35

Maas, Heiko 63
Macron, Emmanuel 115
Maidan Square 37
Maldonado, Guillermo 99
manufacture 75, 77, 91

marginalization 40, 57, 73, 78
masculinity 94
mask 28, 37, 37, 39, 62, 89, 92, 97,
  102, 107, 111–13
Maslow, Abraham 67
"Material-Technical Support Point" 64
MERS 52
#MeToo 27
Middle East 18, 20, 36, 52, 56, 64, 115
migrants 43–7, 56–67, 92, 108
migration 4, 20, 35, 43–6, 48
Milosevic, Slobodan 36
minorities 40, 53–3, 56–7, 81
modernity 61, 124, 126
Modi, Narendra 94
Montenegro 56
Moscow 64; *see also* Russia
Mossad 119; *see also* Israel
Munich Security Conference 64

N95 89; *see also* mask
narrative 24–5, 27–9
nationalist 3, 51–2, 57–8, 61–2, 74,
  77–9; vs. globalist 4
natural disasters 1, 108
Netanyahu, Benjamin 64, 118–19
Netherlands, the 55
New Deal 21
New Delhi 89; *see also* India
New York City 26, 74
New Zealand 94
Nobel, Alfred 10
Nobel Peace Prize 11
nonviolent: movement 1, 36–7, 39, 41,
  73, 81; strategies 36
nuclear 1, 12, 67, 125
nursing 82, 89
Nye, Joseph 62

offenders 28–9
opportunities: gender 90; peace 2–3, 5,
  61–2, 85, 102, 110–11; political 37–8
Orbán, Viktor 56
"Oromo Lives Matter" 40
Overseas Development Assistance 44
Ozerdem, Alpasian 107

Paczynska, Agnieszka 35
Pakistan Channel 125

paleoconservatism 53
Palestine/Palestinians 5, 64, 83, 115–21
Panopto 110
Paris Agreement 63
peacebuilding 3–5, 11, 48, 67, 81,
  85–6, 107, 109, 113, 129–30, 132
peace engineering 109, 113
peacemaking 3, 5, 61–2, 133
PeaceTech Lab 109
Peking University 62
people of color 1, 76, 85–6
Pew Research Center 55, 98
Philippines, the 3, 41
plague 1, 9, 17–19, 38; of Cyprian 131
Poland 39
police brutality 21, 40–1
pollution 24–5, 100
Pompeo, Mike 64
Poor People's Campaign 83
populist/populism 22, 46, 48, 51, 53,
  55, 57
post-corona 2, 22, 61–4, 67, 73, 90,
  119; *see also* post-pandemic
post-pandemic 3, 5, 24, 40, 45, 47, 73,
  101, 109, 113
poverty 81, 83, 92, 125
prayer 10, 117
pre-pandemic 3, 45, 48
Presbyterian 99
"Prima gli italiani" 46
prison 14, 21, 39, 79
propaganda 52, 62
protection 55, 53, 68, 77–8, 84, 91,
  101, 112
protest: against COVID lockdown 75;
  against economic and racial inequality
  17, 73; anti-racist 82; civil 20, 35;
  global 26, 35–40; nonviolent 1; police
  violence 3; use of social media 39;
  violent 3; *see also* #Blacklivesmatter;
  civil rights; Floyd, George
Protestant 97–9, 102–3
Przełóżmy Wybory 39
public health 38, 46–8, 52, 54, 56, 61,
  65–8, 75, 77, 102; measures 19, 42

Qatar 64
Qing, Gao 123
quarantine 20, 40, 65, 74–6, 110

Raheem, Brandon A. 85
Raoult, Didier 66
refugee 14, 24, 26–7, 44–5, 49,
    92–3, 109
religion 98, 100, 103
religious: freedom 58; identity 97;
    organization 5
"repertoire of contention" 36
Republicans 54, 113
Richmond 40
Robber's Cave 116
Roma 56
Romano, Arthur 81
Roosevelt, Franklin D. 10, 21
Root, Elihu 12
root narratives 78
Rubenstein, Richard E. 1, 25, 74, 130
Russia 21, 64–5
"Russia's Security Concept for the Gulf
    Area" 65

Salah, Alaa 37
Santiago 37; *see also* Chile
SARS 19, 52
Saudi Arabia 64
Schirch, Lisa 107
Seattle 74
Sectarian Cold War 62
security: challenges 13, 113; economic
    29, 57, 61, 92; environmental 46;
    food 26; human 1, 14, 53, 108, 113;
    international 67, 119; and peace 66,
    113; regional 126
Security Council 65–7
Serbia 56
Shank, Michael 24
Shin Bet 119; *see also* Israel
Simmons, Solon 1, 9, 78, 130
slavery 38, 77, 82, 98, 108
social cohesion 111–13
social distancing 111
social media 36–7, 39–41, 82, 107–8,
    112, 121
social services 26, 44–5, 77, 84
socio-economic 2, 5, 24, 47, 68, 73,
    100, 109
sociopolitical 5, 98, 102, 108
Söderblom, Nathan 12
South America 39

South Korea 3, 56, 62, 126
Spain 39, 56, 91
Spanish flu 19, 38
Spell, Tony 99
Stearns, Peter N. 17, 74
Stoltenberg, Jens 67
Sudan 36–7
Sung-Won 52
Sustainable Development Goals
    (SDGs) 10, 12
symptom 18, 74

Tahrir Square 37
Taiwan 125
Taylor, Breonna 83
teleconference 67
Texas 27
Thucydides Trap 62–3, 126, 129
Tilly, Charles 22, 35
Time's Up Foundation 91
trade unions 48
trade wars 35
triple crisis 73–9
Trudeau, Justin 28
Trump, Donald J. 46, 56, 62–4, 66–7,
    74–5, 78, 94

unemployment 45–6, 51, 55–7, 74
UNESCO 63
UNFPA 92–3
United Arab Emirates 64
United Nations/UN 5, 10, 11, 14, 61,
    65–8, 91, 93
United Nations Development Program 68
United States 3, 13, 17, 20–1, 25, 35,
    39, 40–1, 54–6, 63–4, 74–6, 81–3,
    86, 89–90, 98–9, 101, 109–10, 112,
    123–9, 131
United States Institute of Peace
    (USIP) 109
Universal Declaration of Human
    Rights 131
Universal Postal Union 63
US Navy EP-3 125

vaccine 2, 35, 46, 48, 63, 79
Vietnam 3, 125–6
violence: cultural 12, 14; domestic 91;
    economic 46; gender-based 92–4;

institutional 11; international 3, 5; physical 26, 29; prevention 85; resolution 43–5; structural 13, 25; systemic 78, 82
VoiceThread 110
Volkan, Vamik 126
von Suttner, Bertha 12
Vucjuk (Bosnia) 92

Walt, Stephen 62
Washington D.C. 109
water 25–6, 65, 92, 109, 113
welfare 13, 21, 98
West Bank 116, 119

Williams, Keshia 89
women 68, 83, 89–95, 110
World Health Organization 20
World War I 19, 21
World War II 10, 62–3, 127

xenophobia 52–3
Xi, Jinping 62

yellow fever 38

Zika 52
Zionism 64
Zoom 83, 110

For Product Safety Concerns and Information please contact our EU
representative GPSR@taylorandfrancis.com
Taylor & Francis Verlag GmbH, Kaufingerstraße 24, 80331 München, Germany